Church Administration
in the
Black
Perspective

Church Administration in the Black Perspective

Floyd Massey, Jr.

and

Samuel Berry McKinney

JUDSON PRESS ®
Valley Forge

CHURCH ADMINISTRATION IN THE BLACK PERSPECTIVE

Copyright © 1976
Judson Press, Valley Forge, PA 19482-0851
Ninth Printing, 1991

Versions of the Bible quoted in this book are:

The Holy Bible, King James Version.

Revised Standard Version of the Bible, copyrighted 1952 and 1971 by the Division of Christian Education of the National Council of the Churches of Christ in the United States of America. Used by permission.

Library of Congress Cataloging in Publication Data

Massey, Floyd.
    Church administration in the Black perspective.

    Bibliography: p. 139.
    1. Afro-American Baptists. 2. Afro-American churches. 3. Church management. I. McKinney, Samuel Berry, joint author. II. Title.
BX6448.M37   254'.06'1   76-9804
ISBN 0-8170-0710-5

The name JUDSON PRESS is registered as a trademark in the U.S. Patent Office.

Printed in the U.S.A.

Appreciation and Acknowledgments

Our families and congregations have sacrificed much that these authors might participate for the past three years in the Martin Luther King, Jr., Program of Black Church Studies at Colgate Rochester/Bexley Hall/Crozer Theological Seminaries, Rochester, New York. To them we express infinite gratitude for their encouragement and adaptability during a period of long-distance "husbanding," parenting, and pastoring. The efficient maintenance of the churches, especially for the duration of this term of study, attests to the existence of effective and integrated administrative plans for which those persons left in charge had been thoughtfully trained.

Thanks must be extended, also, to the assistant and associate ministers and secretaries of these two congregations, through whose competencies direction of administrative organization was coordinated.

In addition, both within and without the Program, indebtedness to educators, fellow ministers, and lay friends must be recognized and expressed. All have become a part of this whole.

Because there do not now exist any suitable nonsexist pronoun substitutes for she, he, her, or him, there is more frequent use of the masculine pronoun than the collaborators desire. Both writers are assiduous proponents of the demise of sex role stereotyping and ask that the reader regard the masculine pronoun, except where there is a specific male antecedent, as strictly generic, inclusive of fe(male) personhood, but with the real knowledge that the black Baptist minister has been and still is generally a male.

As of the eighth printing of this book, the term "African American" has become a preferred designation and may be understood to replace usage of "black" in each instance.

Contents

GOALS OF CHURCH ADMINISTRATION
IN THE BLACK PERSPECTIVE

1. To "equip the saints for the work of ministry" (Ephesians 4:12, RSV).

—leadership by education and training; "integration without preparation equals frustration." [1]

2. To "set at liberty them that are bound." (Isaiah 61:1 and Luke 4:18)

—liberation that secures jobs, housing, education, human rights, i.e., the breaking of all "fetters."

3. "To serve the present age, My calling to fulfil. . . ." [2]

—flexibility to adapt to location, life-style, working and living conditions; the existential nature of decisions people must make.

4. "And O, Thy servant, Lord, prepare a strict account to give." [3]

—accountability for all that is administratively entrusted to one's keeping; assuming responsibility for one's commitments.

5. To reveal the glory of the Lord that "all flesh shall see it together" (Isaiah 40:5).

—sound church administration, demanding excellence at every level of participation and sensitive to human needs resulting in a meaningful future for black children of God.

Preface

The story of an African people, stolen from their native environment, raped in and through the middle passage, enslaved in a "new world," disenfranchised shortly after their emancipation, and denied access to the mainstream of American life, has been recited many times. Another narrative growing out of the same soil, crying to be articulated, is the saga of how these stolen, raped, enslaved, and disenfranchised black people took the crumbs of their existence and produced a "loaf" of hope. The unfolding drama of how these people took the raw material of their lives and organized what has become their strongest institution, the church, must be viewed from the stage of time in proper perspective.

Today there are approximately twelve million black Baptists in the United States. The following chart illustrates the breakdown according to Convention. Not included are the Primitive Baptists and those churches belonging to no Convention. It is no accident that black Baptists comprise the largest single religious group in black communities.

Name of Organization	No. of Churches	Constituent Membership
1. National Baptist Convention of America.	10,000	3,000,000
2. National Baptist Convention U.S.A., Inc.	30,000	8,000,000
3. Progressive National Baptist Convention, Inc.	1,000	1,000,000

Howard W. Thurman, religious philosopher and black church father, speaks to the question of the Baptist denomination being the most popular among the slaves, standing today at the numerical top among black churches:

> I can think of one or two things that are important. . . . it has a tradition of freedom. There is so much local autonomy that any Baptist church can ordain its own men; it's not accountable to anybody beyond the congregation. I would say that its democratic practices in ordination account for the general appeal of the denomination. Not its religiosity, but the fact that in the Baptist denomination any man is as significant as any other. Even the head man is no longer head man when the rest of us *decide* that he *isn't*. And this would have special appeal to people who were terribly circumscribed everywhere else in their world.
>
> These, I believe, are the primary characteristics that made and make the Baptist denomination popular among Blacks, and among whites, too. It seems to me that in specifying them I have described the very genius of the church.[4]

Baptist church administration is predetermined by its high degree of local church autonomy. It is an instrument of self-determination, and self-determination is part of the process of liberation. Therefore, this approach to church administration in black perspective is designed to enable clergy and laity to exercise power creatively and redemptively. The fellowship of followers of Christ, the black church, matures its members to a point of capacity to make decisions and implement them, thus determining and achieving their destiny under God. Policy decisions, elections, budgets, and programs of all kinds are some of the crucial arenas where this maturation may take place. In them, the saints are equipped for the task of ministry in and to the world.

In spite of many recent economic gains experienced in the black community, the black church constituency is comprised of the "organized poor," who lack financial resources and the power to change their condition. Nonetheless, community expectations require the church to meet the needs presented to them. The situation of the black church is similar to that of Jesus of Nazareth when confronted by five thousand hungry men with only five barley loaves and two small fish supplied by a little lad (John 6:9).

"The perennial problem of the Black church is that of facing a large community with a myriad of problems and limited resources to resolve them. Those who administer the Lord's work in Black churches do so with meager means overpowered by overwhelming odds."[5] However, the task of feeding the five thousand has been accomplished by the black church. The leftovers from the same basket have enabled the black church and the community to keep body and soul together.

Within the tradition of inherent freedom, problems sometimes defying solution arise. Often the phenomenon of the free-flowing style of administration is characterized by an ad-hoc-consensus modus operandi, a loose, "free as the wind," freewheeling style of operation not bound by form.

Most administration in Black churches seems to be run by the grace of God and the mercy of the people, without adequate records, permanent paid employees. . . . We have lost many members on the basis that we never use them in the church structures unless they can be used for the personal benefit of the minister and of his administration.[6]

Occasions often surface within the black church, where decisions cannot be based upon rules, regulations, and tradition alone. The exigencies of the situation often demand a flexibility to be led by the "Holy Spirit." The best of both worlds is possible in a style based upon definite rules, building into them a component of flexibility.

For what purpose does one attempt to administer the operation of a church? Is it to pour oil on the machinery or to effect changes in the lives of people? Is it to move from cognitive considerations to attitudinal concerns? Is there a concern for people rather than things? Do we "administrate to liberate"? Do we administer in the spirit of an energized and energizing Christ? The mechanics of church administration are mastered in vain unless they are exercised in a spirit of love and togetherness.

In seeking effective administration, it is assumed that human worth is paramount, affirming the Pauline admonition that all that is lawful is not expedient. The goal assumed in responsible freedom and fulfillment is that all things be done "decently and in order."

Historically, the black church is the only institution that black people control free of white domination. As a result the black church is the custodian of the hopes of black people and often their only hope of gaining administrative experience.

The basic goal of church administration must be the enhancement of people. (See the outline of goals at the opening of this Preface.)

Black Baptist churches are not monolithic. Great variety exists within the family, so much so that a young man, pressured to join a church after leaving his hometown and church, asked, "What do you mean when you say 'unite with another church of the same faith and order'? From what I can see, it may be the same faith, but God knows it's not the same order." Every attempt will be made to look at church administration in the black Baptist church within the experience of the authors.

Although black churches more nearly approximate a classless

society than white churches, for discussion purposes the categories of "mass church," "class church," and "mass-class church" are defined. Black Baptist churches draw their constituents from the "organized poor" of the community. Absent from most black Baptist churches are the "poor-poor," those on the very bottom of any social ladder or scale.

"Mass churches" are those which attract persons in the lower socioeconomic stratum of the black community, although not by any means limited to that grouping. These churches are characterized by large attendance, many colorfully robed choirs rendering music in the "soulful" style, and strong preaching in the black tradition.

"Class churches" are those tending toward middle-class values and norms (white oriented). Membership comes from the upwardly mobile and from some professional ranks, for example, attorneys, physicians, dentists, engineers, and schoolteachers.

A "mass-class" congregation provides a most desirable composite. In such a church the best of all possible worlds is available. Here one can discover a happy marriage of spirit and intellect.

Summary. The black church must be equipped with the administrative tools and skills to enable it to function effectively and efficiently, to be accountable to its constituency within and without its walls, and to deliver a full range of services to its people. As the black church appropriates the necessary technology to be administratively operable, it must, in the words of Lucius M. Tobin, "Redeem technology from its destructive consequences."[7]

Where and when we are critical of the weakness of the black church, it is a lover's quarrel, an attempt to purify it for service in days to come. The black church is our mother and father, our schoolmaster, our base, and our hub: the ground for the development of our being and that of the community.

1
The Tradition of
Lay and Pastoral Relationships

Life in the black churches of today can be better understood by identifying the factors that have had a major influence in their development over the years.

Beginning of the Tradition

The black church was born when a West African stream of consciousness met up with and married, for better or worse, till death they do part, the Judeo-Christian stream of consciousness in the canebrakes, cotton fields, tobacco roads, swamps, river banks, and brush arbors of the southeastern part of the United States.

From Africa the slaves brought a tradition of loyalty to a god who was proved in experience by his effectiveness and his power. Thus, when the slaves were wrenched from their homes and culture and brought to a new situation, their loyalty to their old god came into question. They were vulnerable to the appeal of a new god.[1]

Further, the religious life of the slaves was severely restricted by their masters, even though some were less oppressive than others. Officially, a white person had to be present if they were to meet as a body for worship. Hence, the early black church became an invisible institution which met secretly. In this situation, the lack of a central organization among Baptist churches made it very well adapted to this kind of circumstance.[2]

Such unlawful gatherings of black people were the beginning of the black church. They had to meet at times when they would be safe from the dusk-to-dawn scrutiny of the patrols of the slave owners.[3]

"The slaves soon found that the patrols, for the most part, would turn in just before dawn to rest and would sleep most of the day. They, therefore, came upon the idea of meeting just before dawn in groups and would hold their meetings unmolested" and without the presence of white monitors. "This gave rise to the 'Before-Day-

Prayer-Meetings,'"[4] a practice which still persists along the eastern seaboard and in a few other areas of the nation.

Mays and Nicholson say:

> Relatively early the church, and particularly the independent Negro church, furnished the one and only organized field in which the slave's suppressed emotions could be released, and the only opportunity for him to develop his own leadership. In almost every other area, he was completely suppressed. Thus, through a slow and difficult process, often involving much suffering and persecution the Negro, more than three-quarters of a century prior to emancipation, through initiative, zeal, and ability began to achieve the right to be free in his church. He demonstrated his ability to preach; and this demonstration convinced both Negroes and whites that he was possessed of the Spirit of God.[5]

The late Louis Lomax had this to say about the origin of the black Church after the Emancipation:

> The Negro church was born because Negro clergymen were denied the right to officiate and otherwise hold forth in "white"—actually integrated but white-controlled—churches. The Negro Baptist and Methodist churches are the direct result of overt discrimination. . . . Whenever a people are isolated—by choice or by force, to a limited or total extent— they develop a folkway. In classical terms, there is no difference between the Negro Baptist Church and the Baptist Church proper. In folk terms, however, there is. Not only do we Negro Baptists have a way of preaching and singing, but there is a meaning to our imagery that is peculiar to us.[6]

During the Reconstruction Era many blacks thought the "Kingdom of Liberation" had arrived. Some left the church for greener pastures.

> So many other fields of endeavor opened up for the leaders as a consequence of the attempted policy of reconstruction that the churches actually suffered for the lack of adequate leadership. Although the way was clear for church organization, this work was greatly retarded because so many of the ablest preachers answered the "call of politics." They were constantly faced with new opportunities far more attractive than the ministry. . . .[7]

Swiftly on the heels of President R. B. Hayes's compromise with white southern political leaders, federal troops were removed from the South; the Ku Klux Klan commenced its reign of terror; many blacks were reenslaved under a system of peonage (forced labor/servitude); civil rights were trampled upon; and in 1896, even the Supreme Court declared that education in the southern states would be "separate but equal."

Disappointment and gloom hung heavily over the hearts and hopes of a people desiring to be free. They felt as if a lid had been lowered over their legitimate aspirations.

How was the black church affected by all that had transpired? Wade Hampton McKinney caught the mood of the period:

Finally, the last bitter thrust came for the Negroes. From 1890–1910 an adverse wave of legislation swept over the South disenfranchising the Negroes, thus taking away from them by direct legislation all their Constitutional rights. This had an immediate effect upon the ministry, especially in regards to numbers of the Baptists. The number of ministers in 1890 was only 5,468. By 1906 the total number of Baptist ministers was 17,117. . . .

This series of events made the Negro leaders feel that for some reason the hand of God was against them, that the head of the Churches had come among them and removed the golden candlestick from its place. Although allured and attracted, and at the same time feeling that, as they were the most responsible, it was their duty to enter the field of politics, they now realized that, while they had devoted their time to a commendable work, they had also departed from their first love. Disappointed, they remembered whence they had fallen and consequently returned and began to do the first work. They did the natural thing. . . . The leaders now concentrated their power on the development of the religious and intellectual life of the masses.[8]

The National Association for the Advancement of Colored People was organized in 1909, and the Urban League began its work in 1910. Both of these organizations attempted to make the pitiful plight of black people less deplorable by initiating legal suits to obtain justice through the courts and to prepare those who were leaving the rural South for the realities of a cold urban North.

King Cotton's demise, brought on by the onslaught of the "boll weevil" and the outbreak of World War I, was to affect seriously the lives of countless blacks.

With the Kaiser's German submarines patrolling the Atlantic coastline, American shipping was hampered and the flow of European immigrants dwindled to less than a trickle. With the northern factories needing mill hands and the only available supply of manpower being in the rural South, carload upon carload of rural blacks descended upon Chicago, Cleveland, Columbus, Detroit, Pittsburgh, and other cities to begin life anew in northern communities. Urban church membership substantially increased, and new churches were organized.

Manpower needs being what they were during World War I caused a migratory pattern that was one of movement from the rural South and small towns to the urban North. Between the two world wars of this century, the migration pattern stemmed from the rural South to southern urban areas and from the southern urban areas to northern urban areas.

Eventually, the entry of the United States into World War II accelerated the movement of people, and southern urban areas were "leap-frogged" except as transit points in the tremendous movement of the blacks northward. This northward trend has now leveled off, and blacks are now considering the South as the "land of promise."

How did the black people get to this point? What type of relationships between pastor and people sustained and nurtured them in both rural and urban areas?

Traditional Images of Pastor and Laity

Webster's New World Dictionary defines image as a "mental picture, idea, concept of a person, product, etc., held by the public." What are the images of the rural and urban church syndrome? What are the characteristics of the rural church?

The Rural Church

The rural church was basically a weekend operation. Worship services were held once or twice per month. Although choir rehearsals were not restricted to weekends, church school teachers' meetings, board sessions, and church business meetings were restricted to weekends. Church business meetings, in particular, were usually conducted only on the weekends that the pastor was present for the preaching service.

On the Sundays when the pastor was at another of his churches, the congregation would visit sister churches where a pastor was present. This visitation maintained communication with neighboring congregations and helped to set the spiritual tone for the community.

Small farming communities seemed to have far more churches than they could support. However, efforts either to merge congregations of the same faith and order or to maintain a full-time ministry were met with resistance by the clergy, laity, and, interestingly, many of the leading white citizens.

Some pastors enjoyed the simple preaching ministry of one church per Sunday, per month. They also appreciated the absence of administrative details required of a full-time ministry. Myth has it that some clergy prepared only twelve sermons per year or one per month; the sermon delivered at the fourth Sunday church was "red hot," since it had been refined in three previous presentations!

The laity enjoyed the freedom of not having to support a full-time ministry as well as the freedom to visit other churches on a regular basis. Church officers were happy with the arrangement of the pastor preaching on Sunday and departing Sunday evening or Monday.

The rural pastor was like a revered father in the home, who was loved by his many children, who were on their best behavior when he was at home but who were glad to see him go to work or go away on business so they could relax.

Understandably, some of the leading white citizens did not wish to see a merger of black churches or a full-time ministry for fear of the potential demand for decent, fair, and humane treatment, civil rights, and voting rights. Strong churches led by strong, concerned pastors posed a serious threat to the status quo.

Another characteristic of the rural church centered upon the monthly or semi-monthly visit of the pastor. Legends have emerged around the entertainment of the preacher by the congregation when he came for his "preaching service."

To this day, some black adults claim that their "dislike" for preachers stemmed from their childhood recollections. When the Sunday meal was served, the preacher, they claimed, got the best part of the "gospel bird," that is, chicken—leg, thigh, wing, and breast. All that was left for the children was the "first and last thing that went over the fence," the neck and tail.

The annual "big day," revival/homecoming/baptismal service was a time greatly anticipated, occurring during "laying by time," the middle of August through early September. That was the season when all one could do was wait for the harvest because the planting and cultivating of cotton and the collection of food staples were complete. People came from miles around; families conducted reunions; and a "stem winding" evangelist came in to load up the "mourners' bench," bring sinners to repentance, and hold the largest baptizing of the year.

In addition, the national conventions would convene shortly after the laying by season. Oral tradition claims that the National Baptist Convention began meeting on the Wednesday following the first Sunday in September of each year, for by that time, the church membership had picked, baled, and sold a sufficient amount of cotton to send the pastor and other delegates to the national convention. In fact, three of the major black Baptist bodies, for example, the National Baptist Convention, U.S.A., Inc., the National Baptist Convention of America, and the Progressive National Baptist Convention still convene on the Wednesday following the first Sunday in September of each year.

Characteristic, too, of the rural church worship was its emotionalism. In most situations, the atmosphere of worship has been somewhat modulated.

The Administrative Style of the Rural Pastor

The rural pastor usually served about four churches per month, primarily as preacher. His actual financial sustenance was, however, outside of the church. The itinerant nature of his ministry, though, created a leadership vacuum which the deacons filled. The chairman of the deacon board was often the "de facto pastor." Moreover, the pastor would have to arrange for weddings and funerals via mail and/or long-distance telephone or leave the planning in the hands of the church officers.

Understandably, authority to function in the rural church had to be delegated; responsibility had to be shared. The pastor could maintain his position in such a situation only by his powers of persuasion and by maximizing the role of "spiritual father" at its highest level.

In many instances, excellent rapport existed between pastor and deacons. If the "head deacon" was supportive of the pastor, harmony existed in the church. However, some head deacons had reputations of tyranny far more diabolical than many a pastor with dictatorial leanings could imagine.

One minister remembered his grandfather, the "head deacon" in a small Texas community, who could make or break a minister's career at will. No one, it seemed, crossed him, including the "good white folks." As the sheriff's "deputy for colored people," the head deacon was an untouchable. Rarely was a church meeting called to elect or dismiss a pastor. When he said, "You're the pastor," it was tantamount to election and installation. When he said, "The pulpit's vacant; get out of town as fast as you can," the pastor departed.

Characteristics of the Rural Laity

To understand the nature of Black churches, both rural and urban, one needs to comprehend the role of the tribe/clan both in Africa and in America. African society, says Kofi Asare Opoku, was family oriented, for it was the repository of communal wisdom and heritage.[9] Africans viewed the world through the lens of the tribe/clan. Membership in the tribe was based on blood relationship, adoption, and absorption. The group granted identity and provided coherence and continuity. As a result, there developed a family-structured mind-set which makes understandable the black man's struggle with self-identity apart from the whole.

How did a tribe become a church? It did not! However, slaves brought to America, stripped of possessions, dignity, and purpose for living, might have arrived on these shores empty-handed but not empty-headed. They brought with them the mental cargo of a family-structured society.

Enslaved, dehumanized, demeaned, and divested of most vestiges of self-worth, slaves began to organize their lives around principles that were transferable. The family-oriented mind-set called people from "lostness" to "foundness." Many "po' pilgrims of sorrow," separated from those they knew and loved, were quickly accepted into the family on the new plantation.

Blood relationship established family bonds in Africa, but the slave system so disrupted the African family as to necessitate the development in America of familial groups based on something other than blood.

People were adopted, absorbed, and made one of a family. Older persons were called Uncle and Aunt, terms of familial adoption. Slave owners, misreading this practice, coopted these terms as a device to avoid showing the respect for the older blacks that would have been inherent in addressing them as Mr. or Mrs.

This new family/tribe, established in a strange and alien environment, was not just a social unit. It was both a cultic unit and a religious body, the basis for its structure and organization deriving from Africa where religion and authority to lead came from the group and the ancestors.

For better than one century, very little was done to Christianize slaves. During this period, the slaves kept on establishing new families, without the benefit of white organized religious bodies. In time, however, Christianity spread like a brush fire among the slaves, and family groups aligned themselves with Christianity.

The African mind-set toward family organization, based on blood ties, sailed as the invisible cargo of slave ships, was the genesis of the cultic-based slave family organization in America, was maintained as the slave became Christianized, and evolved into the tribal family church. This family tribal church relationship is characteristic of many contemporary black churches.

Many of the rural churches were family oriented and often the deacons' board comprised the "heads" of these families. The wives of the deacons and older women possessing "spiritual qualities" comprised the deaconesses' or mothers' boards.

Because of the tribal nature of many rural churches, it was often difficult for newcomers to crack the inner circle of church leadership. Rural churches had strong inbreeding tendencies and were pretty much closed-shop operations. Pastors came and went, but the laity kept rolling on with the officers serving as tenured ruling elders.

Another characteristic of the rural laity was its membership in fraternal orders. Miles Mark Fisher graphically illustrates that "camp meetings were similar to the secret tribal assemblies of Negro Africa." [10] He further claims that the native African secret meetings had brought Christianization to American Negroes. They needed the comfort of group fellowship in order to condition themselves to survive under slave situations. Camp meetings and fraternal orders were definite substitutes for the African cults.

There is good reason also to believe that fraternal life among blacks, especially the Masons and the Elks, though practically the same as their white counterparts in many respects, could be designated as black America's version of the African secret societies.

Lodge membership strengthened the self-image of the laity. Fraternal membership bolstered often emasculated male egos. The only places men appeared to be in charge were at church and in the lodge hall.

Furthermore, many blacks learned and mastered the art of procedure, process, and protocol in the lively business sessions of the lodge and church. Avenues of political expression were closed to blacks at one time in the rural south, except in the institutions blacks controlled—the lodge and the church.

Even though leadership circles in the churches were difficult to penetrate, the churches were often oases of hope in deserts of deprivation and despair. The extended family was real. There was always room at the table for one more plate. The uncle who hadn't quite made it had a place to stay; the young girl with a child born out of wedlock, though often forced to make a public apology before the congregation, was included in the family circle. The prodigal son who tried and failed to make it "up North" was received back into the family. The rural church community, in spite of its obvious shortcomings, affirmed and supported the lives of its constituents. A similar support and affirmation was needed as many rural blacks surged northward.

The Urban Church

The mass migrations of blacks from the South to the cities of the North and West, precipitated by two world wars and the Korean conflict, greatly affected the life of urban churches. The patterns of migration were interesting to observe.

During and immediately after World War I, congregations often sent "home" for their pastors, to lead them in their new situations. Some young preachers, upon arrival in northern cities, sought people from their home areas and organized them into churches. After some pastors accepted calls to serve churches in the North, their members would follow them to the new field of service. Moreover, some people from a given area would unite with certain churches en masse. The migratory patterns followed the railroads. Hence, along the eastern seaboard, churches took on nuances characteristic of those in Virginia, North and South Carolina, Georgia, and Florida. In cities like Detroit and Cleveland, the strong influence of Georgia, Alabama, Tennessee, and Kentucky was discernible. Chicago became an extension of the state of Mississippi; St. Louis reflected western Tennessee and Arkansas. The West Coast cities became outposts of Texas and Louisiana.

It was easy in the average, large, industrial city, prior to World War II, to point to a Georgia, Alabama, South Carolina, or Tennessee church. Other congregations were comprised of strong contingents from several states, often in competition with one another and sometimes in constant turmoil.

Existing churches in major cities grew larger and became beehives of activities to assimilate the newcomers, to organize the memberships, and to purchase or reduce indebtedness on church facilities secured from white congregations fleeing the inner cities.

The large and stronger churches had full-time pastors. As smaller churches grew, their pastors forsook other employment to concentrate on the accelerating work load of the church.

In spite of the modifying urbanization of black people, rural church patterns still persisted even after the migrations. Although the city churches conducted worship every Lord's Day, a sizable group of congregants still visited other churches on a given Sunday. The syndrome continued with those who attended church only on the Sunday they ushered or sang or their favorite choir rendered service.

Work patterns in urban areas affected church attendance. Because so many black women, at one time, were employed as domestics and were expected to prepare and serve the Sunday dinner, they could attend only at night. As a result, the Sunday evening worship was the largest attended worship service until other work-related factors intervened. Furthermore, a sizable segment of the black community has been employed by health care institutions, for example, hospitals, rest homes, etc., and thus their church participation has been affected. The same held true for those employed in industries with rotating shifts of the work force. Be that as it may, black churches have experienced and still enjoy large attendance in worship. This is a definite characteristic.

Large numbers of people are involved in the worship experience of black churches. Gigantic usher boards execute their responsibilities, in some instances, with the precision of the changing of the guard at Buckingham Palace, London, England; numerous vested choirs for all age groups sing every Sunday; large deacons' boards, arrayed in black suits and white gloves, plus deaconesses'/mothers' boards, bedecked in white dresses on Communion Sunday, are part of the Sunday drama in most urban black churches throughout the nation. Participation in the life of their church affirms and sustains the sense of "somebodiness" so greatly needed by people victimized by a racist society six days of the week.

Various special days, anniversaries, and celebrations fill out the calendar of the church with great ease. Some organizations have a special program just about every Sunday afternoon at 3:00 P.M. Church, choir, and usher visitations are high moments.

Food service has been basic to the life of black churches. Dinners were and are given for fund-raising and fellowship purposes. At one time, dinner was served every Sunday by groups raising funds or quotas. Food service in recent years has been made available after the early morning worship (8:00 A.M.) and the regular morning worship (11:00 A.M.) to accommodate members who do not wish to take the long ride home and then return for special afternoon or evening affairs.

City churches often serve the Lord's Supper around 4:00 to 6:00 P.M. on a designated Sunday. Although this observance has not been overwhelmingly attended, it has constituted a monthly spiritual "mountain peak." Many churches have literalized the word "supper" and restrict the ordinance to the evening hour. There are churches, however, facetiously accused of observing the "Lord's Breakfast/Lunch," that remember that Jesus said, "As oft as ye eat this bread and drink of this cup, do so in remembrance of me" (see 1 Corinthians 11:24-26). Be that as it may, the elements of the Communion are often carried to the sick and shut-in members monthly or quarterly by the deacons.

In past years, the rural church worship service was considered more emotional than the urban church. Today, however, due to the mass migrations, the urban church has become more emotional and the rural church more staid. There are few "country churches," for they seem to have moved en masse to the large urban centers.

In fact, migrating blacks carried the spirituals northward with them, whereas black, soul, gospel music was created in the urban, industrial, ghettoized communities and has been universalized.

Categorization of black Baptist churches by some pastors has evolved with the following classifications:

Big Church	2,000 members+
Large Church	800–1999
Medium-Size Church	300–799
Small/Little Church	100–299
Tiny Storefront Church	under 100

Furthermore, storefront churches have proliferated on the inner-city landscape. These churches provide a "back home" atmosphere for recent arrivals, nonacclimatized newcomers to urban areas, and function as a halfway house on the way to other churches. They enjoy a high rate of conversions and baptisms.

The Role of the Urban Pastor

The role of the black pastor in an urban setting underwent tremendous metamorphosis. Rather immediately many became full-time rather than part-time in service and were expected to function well on several levels, both in the church and in the community. The black pastor in the city serves two churches, one in the "church house" and one in the community. The support of both is essential to his success in the ministry.

Within the urban church, power struggles have ensued over the role and function of the pastor and officers. Some preachers had trouble adjusting from a rural, once-or-twice-a-month church to a highly structured urban church.

Many church officers, on the other hand, resented a full-time pastor's attempt to run the church when they had been in charge "down home." One veteran pastor, who served a large urban church for over a quarter of a century, felt it was his mission to make "city deacons" out of "country deacons." Likewise, city deacons have hastened the urbanization of many a bucolic cleric. However, long pastorates have been enjoyed by a pastor and his people when tensions have been eased and working relationships understood by all.

Much of the black pastor's time within the church was spent creating an atmosphere where peace and harmony could reign and goals could be planned, executed, and achieved. The pastor was often the arbitrator of major disputes on minor fronts.

In addition, the pastor had to become, overnight, counselor for the home and church; teacher; interpreter of the times; employment specialist; a civic leader with ready answers, not necessarily solutions, to the ills besetting his people; a spokesman, champion, and advocate for the oppressed, defeated, and disenfranchised—a "man for all seasons."

As if this were not enough, the pastor was expected to be a financial wizard, legal counselor, political leader, and the spiritual adviser and evangelist. In short, he was the preacher, pastor, prophet, priest, patriarch, program-promoter, church-name promulgator. He was God's anointed, and representative of the Eternal. The black laity has given no other individual the respect and reverence granted the black clergy.

The black urban church often bordered on being a personality cult and reflected, to a great extent, the personality of the minister. If a pastor exhibited great concern for the welfare of his flock, loved each and every one of the members, was faithful in the discharge of his pastoral duties, and was blessed with the gift of articulation, the people followed him gladly.

The Role of the Urban Laity

Understanding the tribal nature of many black churches, both North and South, is basic to gaining a degree of comprehension of the black religious experience. Like the sister rural church, urban churches were also family oriented. Just as in the South, the deacon boards were comprised of the "heads" of families or "de facto heads" of "tribes" from various southern states or communities within southern states.

Church memberships were easily transferred North and West when persons moved from a tribe-clan church to another very similar to the one they had experienced. People would either search diligently for a church similar to that in their past or refuse to unite with a church because of ties to home.

Acceptance of newcomers, beyond the extension of the "right hand of fellowship," depended largely upon who they were, where they came from, what talents or skills they possessed, and how they moved in and among the membership. Naturally, many people, cut adrift by the pressures of urban life, were content to become lost on the membership roles or just be good "pew" members.

Moreover, the extended family was grafted early on to the corpus of the urban church. People without shelter, rent, food, clothes, and health care received help from the congregation. All types of services were rendered by churches. Responses to appeals for real needs were always tremendous.

Although the laity often placed the clergy on pedestals of glory, indeed, named sons after the pastor, and encouraged their young men to become ministers, in some homes "roasted preacher" was served at every Sunday dinner table. At any rate, all types of folklore have evolved about the black preacher, some commendable, some not. Nevertheless, even when disappointed by a preacher's conduct, the laity still harbored the hope that the preacher would let the "Lord truly use him."

The laity has often been very lenient with its pastors and has forgiven preachers of just about every sin except the failure to preach. Many a pastor has preached his way from "disgrace" back into the "grace" of a living, forgiving, familial fellowship.

Negative images, however, have circulated about the pastoral office even when pastors have walked the razor's edge and have lived circumspect lives. These negative images have been due to misunderstanding, deliberate distortion, and bad experiences of the laity. Because the black preacher belongs to the community, he is available for ridicule. He serves as the people's psychological lightning rod, a possible means of neutralizing their shocks or venting their hostilities.

As previously stated, fraternal life among urban blacks has been of great importance and has had significant impact on the life of the congregation. It should be noted, though, that participation in those organizations was no substitute for the church experience. Fraternal orders provided the laity with an auxiliary system of socialization as well as communication. This system was used quite extensively when churches were in search of a shepherd.

Black college fraternities and sororities, too, have supplied a degree of linkage for black communities and churches. More and more, though, upwardly mobile blacks have now become members of the Rotary, Kiwanis, and Lions service organizations. The masses of blacks who belong to any kind of fraternal organization have been and still are Masons.

Although the laity have supported numerous community groups, they kept their church alive by investing their energies into the organization, meeting untold needs, supporting countless projects and efforts, sustaining themselves and others at life-situational junctures, executing dreams into realities, and finding fulfillment in their own lives, despite deprivations defying descriptions.

The Tradition of a Long Pastorate

"There is a very close similarity," claimed Kofi Opoku, "between the long pastoral tradition of Black Baptist pastors and the lifetime reign of the West African chiefs of Ghana."[11] What was true of Ghana is applicable to other parts of Africa as well. He continued by declaring that the basic ingredients for a lifetime of service for both the black Baptist pastor and African chief are: productivity in common ventures, faithfulness in observance of the details of the ritual and culture of the group, growth in the group, and wisdom in the exercise of justice for all.

Churches are the lengthening shadows of their leaders. The long pastorate is the natural outgrowth of the father-figure image. The father-figure image syndrome, basic to the expectations of the black religious heritage, was rooted in Africa and the Bible. The lack of a male presence in many homes added to the expectation that the minister be a father to the fatherless. In many instances the black pastor organized the church; made numerous sacrifices for the institution; and served several generations—baptizing, marrying, and burying members of the same family; and made contributions in all areas of the total life of the church and community.

Because the black pastor does not change pastorates every three to five years, he can ill afford to be the silent partner in the marriage of pastor and people. The nuptials of pastor and people cannot be a shot-gun affair, nor can the pastor be a kept eunuch of a ruling elite.

Moreover, black pastors, generally speaking, cannot aspire to the bishopric as an upward move out of the pastorate. As a result, the average black Baptist pastor must, of necessity, develop a program.

Many clergy have accepted denominational and ecumenical positions, including those on campuses and in community-oriented programs, but these brethren tend to move back into the pastorate as soon as the right opportunity for a church presents itself, or they receive an "offer they cannot refuse."

For some reason, the black laity has difficulty with a cleric "who can preach but who is not in the 'pasturage,'" a colloquial modification of pastorate. A pastor is often effective in other roles only if he maintains a church as a base of operation. For example, the presidents of three black Baptist Conventions are pastors.

A clergyman who enjoyed a successful pastorate of several years left his charge to participate in a newly emerging ministry. He, along with other ministerial friends, was invited to dinner at the home of one of his former parishioners. The man of the house, to the surprise and shock of all gathered about the festive board, emphatically declared, "I'm going to ask Reverend _____, who is still in the ministry, to ask God's blessings upon the food." The "former pastor" returned to the pastorate as soon as the right opportunity opened.

There are definite advantages to a long pastorate: continuity and stability; projection and completion of long-range goals; development of a sense of family and community; preparation and strengthening of the laity; capability for cultivating an entourage of "sons in the ministry"; a base of operation for community development.

On the other hand, some of the weaknesses of a long pastorate are: tendency toward deterioration of program and attrition in membership toward the end of a pastorate, because the leader stops growing; entrenchment of a tightly knit ruling elite; insecurity of an aging pastor and fear of younger men and new programs; failure to plan for an orderly transition from one regime to another.

To substantiate the tradition of long pastorates, a random sampling of the length of pastorates of black Baptist ministers was taken. The data were collected from the Faculty and Fellows in the Martin Luther King, Jr., Program in Black Church Studies, from ministers throughout the nation, and from personal knowledge.

The following summarizes the data collected on 253 black Baptist pastors in 45 cities across the United States:

Pastoral Duration in One Church

Years of Service	Number of Pastors
60 or more	2
50 to 59	12
40 to 49	29
30 to 39	67
20 to 29	143
Total	253

The random sampling substantiated the tradition of lengthy pastoral tenure among black Baptist ministers. In like manner, black ministers in the Pentecostal tradition, by and large, taste the "sweet fruits" of a long pastorate.

In contrast, true to the connectional polity of Methodism, black Methodists in the United Methodist Church and the all-black Methodist bodies, for example, African Methodist Episcopal, African Methodist Episcopal Zion, and Christian Methodist Episcopal Churches, are subject to the "godly wisdom of the bishop." Only in rare instances does one discover a black Methodist with a long pastorate. Be that as it may, the tradition of a long pastorate exists among all other blacks who are in non-Baptist churches.

The black clergymen in the basically all-white denominations generally have excellent educational preparation for the ministry.

However, racism has denied them vertical mobility through the "chairs of office" within their denominations and has locked them into lengthy pastorates. Because of their long tenure, the churches they serve are some of the most stable in their denomination, even though caught in a swelling tide of Blackness with its expectations and goals.

The following summarizes a random sampling of the long pastoral tradition of black churches in predominantly white denominations (the Episcopal; Presbyterian, U.S.A.; and United Church of Christ.):

Pastoral Duration in One Church

Years of Service	Number of Pastors
40 or more	4
30 to 39	8
20 to 29	18
Total	30

Father-Son Tradition

That the son of an African chief succeeds his father on the throne is not unusual. The line of succession to many of the African thrones is not restricted to royal families, however.

In like manner, it is not unusual for sons of black Baptist pastors to succeed their fathers. This practice of succession, though not automatic, is woven into the fabric of the black church.

Buried deep in the heart of most black preachers is the hope that the Lord will "call" at least one son into the ministry. A quick look at the Martin Luther King, Jr., Fellows in Black Church Studies revealed that eleven of the twenty Fellows were sons of ministers. Four of the eleven were third-generation clerics. One was the grandson of a preacher.

Some of the father/son combinations have received wide fame. A random sampling of the father/son tradition in black Baptist churches produced this listing, which is far from complete.

Adam Clayton Powell, Sr.*	Abyssinian: New York, N.Y.
Adam Clayton Powell, Jr.*	
Martin Luther King, Sr.	Ebenezer: Atlanta, Ga.
Martin Luther King, Jr.*	Co-pastor
A. D. Williams King, Sr.*	Co-pastor
J. C. Austin, Sr.*	Pilgrim: Chicago, Ill.
J. C. Austin, Jr.	
W. H. Gray*	Bright Hope: Philadelphia, Pa.
W. H. Gray, Jr.*	
W. H. Gray, III	

Marshall L. Shepard, Sr.*	Mt. Olivet: Philadelphia, Pa.
Marshall L. Shepard, Jr.	
Elijah J. Echols, Sr.*	First Shiloh: Buffalo, N.Y.
Elijah J. Echols, Jr.	
D. W. Hill*	Second Mt. Sinai: Cleveland,
Luther F. Hill	Ohio
F. D. Haynes, Sr.*	Third: San Francisco, Calif.
F. D. Haynes, Jr.*	
E. W. Perry, Sr.*	Tabernacle: Oklahoma City,
E. W. Perry, Jr.	Okla.

(*=deceased)

So deep is the feeling that a son should have the "right" to succeed his father as pastor that prospective candidates for a vacant pulpit will often not permit their names to be considered until the position and interest of the son are known.

The reasons for which congregations accept sons to succeed fathers as pastors are understandable:

1. Continuity—known entity versus unknown entity.
2. Easier transition—leadership succored in the tribe/clan/church.
3. Security for the congregation.
4. The "royal lineage" mind-set.
5. Consideration of the son as a worthy successor.
6. Designation by father of son as successor.

On the other hand, and certainly just as understandable, is the fact that many sons seek pastorates other than one previously held by their father in order to establish their own distinct identity, to make a clean break with the past, or because of the intervention of circumstances. Established, though, is the fact of the father/son heritage in the black church.

Views of Retirement

Black pastors, by and large, have felt they were called by God to serve until death. Clergymen of an earlier generation did not believe in retirement, for their call was for "life." It was considered better to "wear out than to rust out"; therefore retirement of pastors has tended toward resistance by both clergy and laity.

Black church membership is like the African family. One is an equity-holder, either born into it or voluntarily "buying" into it. There is a relationship in the clan/family/church which differs from that of the preacher-as-hired-hand attitude of so many white churches. Retirement is resisted by the black laity because it breaks and disrupts that family relationship.

Many African societies, especially the Akan society found in Ghana, are based on obligation and not on individual rights. One born into the African/Akan family, which includes the Ashanti, Fanti, and Twi ethnic groups, receives inherent rights which are neither merited nor earned. These rights, however, impose obligations. (What has been said of Akan society may well be true for other ethnic groups as well.) K. A. Opoku states:

> One is a person in relationship to others. Personhood apart from others is ludicrous, for mutuality and interdependence are cornerstones upon which the Akan society is constructed. In the exercise of one's obligation one enjoys one's rights. One does not enjoy rights if the society does not exist.
>
> Upon death, one becomes an ancestor and this carries an obligation to the living. Western culture needs to understand that the Akan culture believes strongly in ancestor reverence, not ancestor worship. Because ancestral obligation moves from time into eternity, there is an unending, continuous community of the living and the dead.[12]

There is reason to believe that the idea of the African family has been unconsciously kept alive in traditional black churches in the United States.

In traditional African/Akan society there is no dichotomy between the sacred and the secular. Religion and life are intertwined. The pastor/chieftain's duties cannot be limited to "spiritual" responsibilities. Every chief has a religious function to perform in addition to political duties. Moreover, every priest is an herbalist, that is, a physician, as well as a spiritual leader.

The role of the spiritual leader is so enmeshed in the total life of the group that retirement could render that society dysfunctional.

A heritage of seniority accrues because of faithfulness. Longevity affects the life-style of a church in relation to its administration. Discontinuity results from the rupture of relationships.

To be reckoned with, too, is the fact that not very many black pastors have accumulated a nest egg to sustain them during their years of retirement. Even when they are able to retire comfortably, second thoughts plague them. J. Raymond Henderson, pastor-emeritus of Second Baptist Church, Los Angeles, retired in 1963. Although he was financially able to live adequately in retirement, he has since expressed regrets, urging pastors not to retire unless ill health requires it. On the other hand, John M. Ellison, chancellor of

Virginia Union University, Richmond, Virginia, an outstanding exponent of retirement, continues to urge pastors to plan years ahead to retire at age sixty-five. Contradictory to this, though, is the fact that he is in his eighties and is still teaching. "Veneration of age is part of the Black heritage," proclaims Thelma Adair.[13] Out of the African milieu comes respect for the elder members of a group. Because blacks have been grossly affected by "social inevitability," a tremendous number, especially males, do not begin to realize their full potential or approximate their true capabilities until they near or reach their retirement years.

While retirement is still in the experimental stage for the black pastor, the advent of Social Security and the pension plans of predominantly white denominations and insurance companies have caused some pastors and churches to begin to look at retirement more favorably.

However, the automatic retirement of the black laity from their job communities is affecting the attitude of black church memberships toward retirement and portends a very interesting future for all concerned. In the meantime, many concur with O. L. Sherman, who powerfully proclaimed from his wheelchair, "You can set a bishop down, but you can't retire a preacher."[14]

2
Traditional Patterns of Power in Black Baptist Churches

Power is defined in *Webster's New World Dictionary* as the "ability to do or act—vigor; force; strength; authority; influence." One has power who, possessing authority and influence, acts vigorously from a position of strength to bring about change or achieve a desired goal. Any investigation of power arrangements in black Baptist churches has to commence with the office of the pastor.

The Office of the Pastor

All the power/authority exercised by the black pastor is that granted by the congregation under God, the eternal head of the church. The pastor's role, his function, and his style of operation directly affect the success or failure of the congregation.

Why is the role/function/style of operation of the pastor so important? A young woman said this to the pastor when asked to unite with a church: "When considering a church, I take a very close look at the pastor and try his spirit by my spirit. God is the same and the people will act up the same way everywhere; so, if I dig his style, that is where I'll place my membership."

Several years ago the late Ira De Augustine Reid, eminent sociologist, conducted a very extensive study on the educational background of "Negro" Baptist ministers. One of the many questions posed related to laity expectations of the minister.

> I asked ministers and laymen from all sections of the country to give their opinions on the type of preacher desired by the Baptist people. They all seem to agree on several requisites, namely:
>
> 1. He must have a divine call to the ministry.
> 2. He must be able to mix and mingle with the people.
> 3. He must believe what he preaches.
> 4. He must be a good organizer.
> 5. He must be able to make himself heard and must present his material in an understandable manner.[1]

Spiritual Leader

In West Africa, religious leaders were considered elders. The elders' authority rested on a religious foundation because they represented the community before the ancestors, the living dead. The respect that black preachers had in some quarters was carried over from the African tradition that the chief had religious duties to perform as head of the clan.[2] As head of the church, the black minister's divine call mandated spiritual leadership to a people frustrated in earthly power.

In part, that spiritual leadership had to be communicated through the preaching of the gospel in "basic black." Basic black meant articulation in the black idiom that lifted people from where they were to where they had to be. Inherent in basic black was mass appeal to all groups within the black Christian religious community.

The following is a written statement given to Ira De A. Reid for his study of black Baptists:

> It might be justly said that the Negro Baptists want a preacher who can reach the will of man through both his intellect and his feelings. However, if the preacher does not have a two-fold approach, the people will settle for one who has an emotional approach as over against the intellectual approach.[3]

Furthermore, the black lay person has considered the pastor a father, regardless of the leader's age. It is not unusual for an eighty-year-old church member to tell a young pastor, "You are the father of us all." And to the pastor's wife these words would be uttered, "You are our mother."

The fatherly image of the pastor has been linked to that of a shepherd. The shepherd led, fed, protected, corrected, and supported the flock. For black people, the shepherd was the pastor; the flock was the congregation; and the sheepfold was the church building.

The spiritual nature of the office of pastor has caused many black ministers to consider themselves servants of God, servants of the church, and servants of the community. The desire to assume the role of servant has, however, been crushed by the people's insistence that the pastor assume a stern and lofty role and demeanor. The servant often had to become the firm and strong master, neither servile nor subservient.

Pastors secure within themselves have never required lofty perches from which to minister to their flocks. They are free to be themselves as well as to be the "Eternal's handymen." For example, F. Douglas Ferrell, a pastor in Los Angeles, California, actually constructed the church edifice with membership assistance, built his own home, and assisted many of his congregants in the construction of their own domiciles.

Building upon the solid foundation of spiritual leadership, the black preacher validates his credentials. As a result, he can follow truth wherever it leads him and can provide sustenance for the flock over which the Holy Spirit has placed him.

Strong Person

The pastor is commander-in-chief by virtue of his call by God and the people, and often by virtue of his training. For the pastor not to assert himself is a sign of weakness. The "humble" pastor in past years often found the reins of leadership removed from him. Thus, the black pastor took full control, using his charm, mystique, charisma, and skills to keep from being considered ineffectual and weak. His authority to command came from God. "I am that I am" sent him (see Exodus 3:14). In some churches, the officers and members did not open a window without order or permission from the pastor. Laymen have often been heard using the remark, "I'd rather be asked up than down." The traditional black pastor was used to *giving orders* and seldom took orders. To take orders tends to be considered a sign of weakness.

When and how does a pastor receive the reins of power in a church? Gardner C. Taylor says that the new minister *becomes* pastor as time moves on. When elected and installed, he is not truly the pastor. He *becomes* the pastor as his ability becomes respected and he grows in the hearts of the people.[4] To become pastor means that some officers release authority. The power to lead a congregation is not a natural concomitant of the call. The right to lead must be earned and, improperly used, can be taken away.

People invest power in the leadership of the pastor. He needs the wisdom to know how much power he has and when and where he received it.

The Ashanti in Ghana had a well-developed "enstooling and destooling" process for chiefs. The one enstooled could remain on the stool (seat of authority) as long as one led the people positively and enabled them to achieve their goals. Whenever the "enstooled" ceased to lead positively, the Ashanti had elaborate ways of "destooling" a leader.[5] What has been said of the Ashanti could be true of other tribal groups in Africa. There is reason to believe that this enstooling and destooling process found its way into black Baptist churches.

Gardner C. Taylor again claims that "some churches have to be built, but most had to be won by the pastor." The late Miles Mark

Fisher once said to a fledgling pastor, "Young man, don't use your influence until you get it."[6]

The late Wade Hampton McKinney had this to say to his son who was about to embark on his first pastorate:

> While helping my father plow the land we were sharecropping in Northeast Georgia, he told me to bring the wagon from under the tree out to where he was working in the field. This was my first chance to drive the team of mules. No sooner was I in the driver's seat than the mules bolted. The wagon overturned. My father pulled me from under the wagon and said, "I should whip you, but you've been whipped enough." The wagon was loaded with manure. Then he gave me some advice which has stood me in good stead down through the years. "The next time you drive anything, take the reins before you grab the whip."[7]

Part of the strength of a pastor has been caught up in the idea that he is like all men; yet he is at the same time something different.

A church officer once said to Sandy F. Ray, eminent Brooklyn pastor, "You are a man just like I am." Pastor Ray replied, "Since we both know we are men, let us examine the phrase, 'just like I am.' How did you get to Brooklyn?" "I came up here to work during the war," was the reply. "And how did I get here?" Pastor Ray asked. "Oh, we called you and brought you here," was the reply. "And you are a man, just like I am?"[8]

Moreover, the pastor's strength has been basic to sound governance of the corporate life of the congregation. He has to understand the power he has. He is required to walk a tightrope in the exercise of power and authority by leading the people with a sense that the power he utilizes was delegated to him under the watchful eye of the eternal God. Far too often a black pastor has been called a dictator unjustly. He is not a dictator, but his role has to be clearly understood in light of the congregation in which he has been called to function. When a black pastor tells someone to do something, he is not speaking for himself but for the congregation.

Elliott J. Mason was asked on one occasion, "Do you believe in the strong pastor or strong democracy in the black church?" "It is not a question of either/or, but both/and," he replied. "A strong pastor maintains democracy. He keeps things in order, minimizes power grabs, maintains the balance of power. When someone or a board calls the pastor a dictator, it simply means that the pastor is keeping that person or board from dictating."[9]

In crisis situations, the strong pastor remains calm. He knows he can reach more people on any given Sunday than his opposition. The strong pastor never minimizes opposition, but seeks to neutralize it.

"Make sure that the opposition is fighting the church," O. Clay

Maxwell, Sr., was heard to say. "Never let it appear he's opposing you, but the church."[10] "If you kill a person who is opposing you," elucidated Wade H. McKinney, "he will have a resurrection. But if the people kill him, he is dead, indeed."[11]

The strong pastor can smile in the face of groundless opposition and can overlook the statement of a deacon who was famous for saying, "Let us support the pastor's program; if it succeeds, he succeeds, and if it fails, he fails."

A strong, fatherly, concerned pastor inspires people to follow his and their Christ, not with strong-armed tactics, but by loving them into basic Christian discipleship.

Administrative Leader

The administrative style of the pastor has determined the success or failure of the congregation. His style has had to harmonize with the pace and rhythm of the congregation.

In the black church, it is exceptional for persons to speak or meet with officers or members without the pastor's permission. Likewise, in the villages of West Africa, no one would go to visit without first stopping by the home of the chief. This perhaps seems like dictatorship, but in reality it makes for less confusion. In the matter of fund raising or program alteration, experience dictates that the pastor be consulted, since those are responsibilities for which the pastor is accountable. The black church has its own way of being democratic. Whenever a pastor or lay person "gets out of line," the people handle him or her appropriately.

Sandy F. Ray, earlier quoted, said that if a black Baptist pastor told the denominational leader his congregation would give a certain amount to an objective, then it would be forthcoming, but if the pastor said he had to meet with his officers, that meant the pastor was not planning to contribute. Elliott Mason, again, related that when he began his Los Angeles pastorate, the officers and members came to him to ask one question after another regarding every activity from the big building program down to uniforms for ushers. They would not move until the pastor told them in what direction God was directing him, and much of this surprised him. But he said he finally decided if they kept asking, he had better tell them!

The black church demands that the pastor lead. Even if he wanted to lag behind in humble fashion, the people would push him to the front of the army and crush him with criticism if he did not move them forward. A pastor, failing to give forceful leadership, strikes the death blow to his own program. Lay people always want to know,

"What is your program?" Of course, that is not to say that they are ready to follow. It may have been to learn what they were to oppose, but the culture insists on prominent leadership from its pastor. As a consensus-oriented people, consensus may have been to determine if leadership was adequate and if one was the pastor or not. Milton K. Curry, Jr., stated: "Black people will not run over their leadership: They will move them first."[12] This is not to state that the pastor has to do everything. He knows that it is better to put nine men to work than to attempt to do the work of nine men.

In the black church, the pastor usually presides over the combined official board meetings and the congregational meetings. He is also responsible for the instruction of officers and teachers. The black church is more harmonious in its deliberations when its spiritual leader presides, although lay persons have presided.

It should be noted that the black pastor has traditionally tended to feel protective of those members who are unfamiliar with E. T. Hiscox's *The New Directory for Baptist Churches* and *Robert's Rules of Order,*[13] for those versed in the use of these volumes have often used them as parliamentary weapons against the unversed, rather than as aids. In addition, every big project initiated calls for a "financial vote" of confidence from the people. Black congregations support the program only when they admire the pastor, or when necessity is placed upon them.

The Community Leader

The African chief attempted to meet the community's spiritual and social needs by leading his community in its fight against evil. The needs of the African community were interpreted for "this world" and were not otherworldly in orientation, although West Africans believed in the afterlife in which they became ancestors.

The here-and-now orientation followed the African into his Western servitude. He detested slavery and rebelled, claimed James H. Cone, "with every ounce of humanity in him. . . . Most used the church as a platform for announcing *freedom* and *equality*."[14]

The pre-Civil War preacher and church were caught up in the struggle to be free and to survive. As a result, most of the slave insurrections were led by preachers, such as Nat Turner, Gabriel Prosser, Denmark Vesey, and a bevy of others. These insurrections engendered in whites the need for vigilant monitoring of slave gatherings. To prevent such insurrections, two white persons had to be present during a worship service to censor what the black preacher proclaimed.[15]

Following the Civil War, the black churches and their preachers, according to James Cone, accommodated themselves and their people to the status quo.[16] In the middle 1950s, Rosa Parks' refusal to give up her seat on a Montgomery, Alabama, bus was the shot heard around the world, destined to arouse the sleeping "black giant" from his slumber, to seize the time. The Montgomery struggle for human dignity catapulted Martin Luther King, Jr., into prominence and ultimate martyrdom. "Mike" King brought glory again to an historic role which is part and parcel of the expectations that swirl about the black preacher.

Because the pulpit in the black church is the only truly "free" pulpit in America, black people expect judgment to begin at the house of the Lord. The financial support of the black preacher comes directly from the people, thereby freeing him both to give unfettered interpretation to the times and to affect the times as both priest and prophet.

While Martin Luther King, Jr., holds a place of deep affection in the hearts of most prideful black Americans, it must be remembered that he was preceded by a great throng of unknown and unsung heroes of the faith, who made his thrust a reality.

From the shoulders of his own father, Martin Luther King, Sr., and Vernon Johns, his immediate predecessor at Dexter Avenue Baptist Church, Montgomery, Alabama, Martin Luther King, Jr., emerged to stamp his great deeds indelibly upon the scrolls of time.

Unfortunately, after King's assassination, vicious attacks of just about every type were leveled at many clergy who, like King, had been active in the struggle for human dignity in their respective communities. Fortunately, however, most of the clergy emerged from the struggle "bloody but unbowed."

One of the struggle-scarred brothers was heard to proclaim:

No one in this or any community can speak for me who:
—pimped off the suffering of my people;
—talked black but slept white;
—talked revolutionary rhetoric out of one side of his fat mouth while he sold his people and community out from the other side of his mouth;
—doesn't believe in Jesus Christ;
—always wanted the church to support his ventures but refused the adventure of the church into the precincts of his very soul.[17]

Again, the black preacher and the church he serves have been the only institutions in the black community with the content, continuity, concern, capacity, and compassion to deliver liberation to the people.

General Officers

Deacons

Deacons, along with the pastor, have enjoyed the distinction of occupying the only two scriptural positions in the church. Some deacons consider themselves the church's spiritual fathers, ruling elders who serve and assist the pastor in the shepherding of the flock and, as a rule, have been basically loyal to the pastor and the church, in spite of pressures brought on them to function differently.

On the other hand, there have been deacons and other officers who felt it their solemn and sworn duty to *protect* the congregation *from* the pastor. Others considered themselves as employer and subsequent boss of the pastor.

Most deacons have recognized the importance of maintaining the integrity of the institution. Maintaining the integrity of the institution was interpreted as the support or trust given to a position or recommendation presented by other members who have done "their homework," even if one has not heard the proposition previously.

In the average black Baptist church, the deacon board is the power board. Generally, if this board is part and parcel of the "With-the-Pastor Club," the only way that church can go is up.

Often, however, the deacon board can be racked with dissension because of latent ambitions, power struggles, or the eclipse of one clique and the ascension of another clique.

Deacons have usually risen in influence in the church according to seniority, pastoral appointment, educational opportunities, specialized training, "mother wit," "jungle smarts," "moxie," self-assertion, or ability to perform well at several levels. Deacons and all other board personnel are, according to black church understanding, church officers in a board context.

Trustees

Many churches have, unfortunately, permitted the dichotomization of the type of persons to serve on the diaconate (boards of deacons and deaconesses) and on the board of trustees. Older ministers felt that every issue that could conceivably be brought before the church was either spiritual or material. If it was spiritual, it was referred to the deacons. If it was material, it was referred to the trustees.

Sometimes, conflict between the two boards ensues. It is to the dismay, disgust, and pique of many a black church trustee to learn that as the pastor and deacons go so goes the church.

Often there are trustees who feel it their duty to stand between the pastor and people, not understanding that black congregants disallow intercessory unavailability to the pastor.

By and large, however, black churches owe a great debt of sincere gratitude to church trustees who have given unstintingly of themselves, their time, talent, and treasure to care for the church over, above, and beyond the call of duty. Most ministers have enjoyed happy relations with those who handled the resources committed to them by the people of God.

Other Officers

Depending upon the church in question, church clerks have been invested with a great deal of power, due to the crucial record-keeping function inherent in the office.

A church treasurer and/or church financial secretary have had power, too, because it has been their responsibility to determine whose voucher would be honored and which debts and creditors would be paid at any given time. Money is power, and those who receive or disburse it automatically possess power, defined and circumscribed though it is.

Auxiliary Groupings

The Negro church operates through small fellowship groups. These groups can be roughly divided into three classes: (1) Service Groups—such as choirs, usher boards, gospel choruses, flower guilds, etc.; (2) Fellowship Groups—such as men's clubs, women's auxiliaries, missionary societies, etc.; (3) Interest Groups—such as church school, state organizations, age group circles, etc. These groups, in spite of my arbitrary categories, have as their primary mission the financial support of the institution. It is common for a single church to have twenty-five or thirty small bank accounts in as many banks in a major large city. Most often, each group is duplicated in an organization for children and youth. In a single church there will be a senior choir, a youth choir, and a children's choir. This multiplicity of groups affords an opportunity for "everybody to be somebody." [18]

The pastor who tackles the task of centralizing all the auxiliary treasuries into one church treasury has often had his days numbered and full of trouble. His successor, however, generally benefits from his sacrifice to place all funds under bond.

Of significance is the fact that leaders of auxiliaries have served long terms and gained power by virtue of years in office. Experience or skill is respected. Because capability in music has been a skill needed and greatly respected by the black church, the choir director has generally been given high regard and is often an autonomous authority responsible only to the pastor. Church officers and music committees give circumspect and often permissive attention to the requirements of the church musician.

The questions of power which usually emerge from the auxiliary groups deal with:

—the parameters of participation, rights, and responsibilities of the groups to the church;

—the sanctity of their special days;

—the use and handling of their funds.

What are some of the basic black church auxiliaries?

Music Department

The Music Department has been called the war department of the church simply because there is more potential for conflict among groups that meet often than among those that don't. Frequency of interaction often makes groups organized to engender creative tension repositories of degenerative tension.

The organist, pianist, and/or choir director are usually selected by the pastor or recommended by the pastor to the music committee. Where there is a minister of music, that person clears all music personnel through the pastor.

Choirs have elected officers, purchased music and robes, conducted special events, and participated in visits and exchanges too numerous to count. These activities have not only enriched the church, but also have created another arena for participatory growth for its constituents.

Usher Board

Ushering in the black church has been far more important an activity than the same role in its white counterpart. The ushering units of the black church are often large, departmentalized, and paramilitary. Although ushers march with soldier-like precision, guard entrances and exits zealously, direct the traffic into the sanctuary and parking lots as policemen, ushers also sponsor programs and purchase uniforms for themselves and equipment for the church building. Like choirs, they have senior, junior, and youth usher boards.

Many of the usher boards sponsor a nurse's unit and equip a "recovery room." Again an arena for service development, fellowship, and growth has been created.

Church School and Baptist Training Union

Church attendance was at one time directly related to church-school attendance. Some church schools with large, adult classes and well-departmentalized instruction for children and youth often rival the church itself.

The superintendent in some churches is the "pastor" of the church school. In some instances, the church school is better organized and conducted than the church. Because the church school is the major training arm of the church, potentially or actually it is a tremendous power base.

Never a serious rival of the church school, the Baptist Training Union (successor to the BYPU, Baptist Young People's Union) has been the Sunday evening training arm of the church, which sometimes provides the bait to bolster the evening worship hour. The degree of power this group exercises varies with the people involved.

Women's Work

Women's societies are usually fairly calm and disciplined. But here again, a power pattern is at work which moves from the president of the society to the church kitchen. The greatest missionary work is administered through the women's society. The largest representation in the Convention is from the women's society. Among the women there is found the sponsoring of workshops, study groups, church beautification programs, teas, style revues, banquets, and dinners.

"The Negro church is a reflection of the matriarchal society which is common to Negro family life," Charles Sargent declares. "Although the leading officers (preachers and deacons) are limited to men, it is the women who dominate the life of the churches. Because the female," Sargent continues, "is the dominant force in family life, she also has the responsibility of maintaining the community which is evident in the church." [19]

Reporting on the 1971 session of the NCBC (National Committee of Black Churchmen) held in a church in Chicago, Illinois, Cornish Rogers described the predicament of the pastor refusing to allow a woman delegate to speak from the pulpit. In explaining that the church had voted into being such a regulation, and that 80 percent of his members were women, the pastor proclaimed that in his church *"the women rule and the men preside."* [20]

Many black women, who believe in "equal pay for equal work," claim that they could take over the church if they so desired. However, they recognize the need for viable images of black males and support the church which keeps the men "out front."

In the average black church there is a women's block of power that functions as a prime mover. In some churches it might be the women's society; in others the deaconesses' or mothers' board or young matrons. Every pastor owes much of his strength in a church to the support of the women.

Men's Fellowship

The laymen usually organize for fellowship. In some instances, effective church cleaning and repair days are observed. Moreover, they participate in work days at denominational group sites. Unfortunately, the brotherhood organizations of the church have not been as viable as they should have been, for many black men have not yet recognized the power potential within them.

When a father says, "As for me and my house, we will serve the Lord," the kingdom of God moves a little closer toward fulfillment. Whenever the male says that he and his family will support the church, real progress takes place. When men contribute, it is always better than the wives "pinching off part of the grocery money" for support of the church.

Other Cultural Factors
View of the Bible as Textbook

The Bible has usually been the textbook for black churches, and the New Testament the guide and norm for Baptist church government. Other manuals have not been considered helpful, because often by the time the guidance of a manual was sought, a crisis situation which was beyond resolution had developed.

One's administrative style has to be scriptural, but not supported by proof texts. Older pastors knew to what end to use the Scripture in church administration. They knew it was good for doctrine, reproof, and training.

The Bible is, however, not a vehicle through which to "nitpick" in order to find a text to justify a given or intended action. Nor is it a cookbook that provides recipes for every situation. Church administration should be characterized by the New Testament's sense of order and its spirit, and it should be conducted on the principles of need, service, and love.

Troubling questions have surfaced occasionally which demand attention. Is the democratic nature of the church a biblical category? Was participatory democracy exercised and experienced in the early church? How much church administration is based on biblical models and not those of contemporary business and politics? What place does the Holy Spirit have in church administration, or is it basic to the New Testament church? The answers then and now require considerable cultural insight.

Reverence for Age

Old people were not useless in traditional African society, for they were considered the repository of community wisdom. For Africans, wisdom was practical and experiential rather than theoretical. However, conflict between wisdom and knowledge has emerged in Africa, according to K. A. Opoku. For him, wisdom was practical, growing out of experience. On the other hand, knowledge was the utilization of the educational process. There can be theoretical knowledge but not theoretical wisdom. Wisdom was acquired by becoming immersed in culture and the ways inherent in it. Being an elder meant that one must conduct oneself in ways conducive to garnering respect. Respect was not automatic.

An Akan proverb helps to illustrate the responsibility age had to oncoming generations if it indeed expected to be venerated.

> "An elder does not roast a hot stone and
> place it in the hand of a child." [21]

If an elder left food on his plate, it meant that he recognized the presence and worth of children. Furthermore, it was not considered a sign of disrespect to eat from the plate of an elder; hence, this proverb was fraught with much significance:

> "A greedy elder washes his own dishes." [22]

Moreover, the elder had the responsibility of pouring libations to the ancestors. By pouring a drink on the ground and calling upon the ancestors, the elder kept them informed of current events. This was known as pouring a libation.

Instruction to the young was given by the elders who had both the honor and obligation of passing their wisdom on to the younger generation. These Akan proverbs provided helpful insights:

> "When the buttocks of an elder grow thin, it goes
> into those of the younger generation."

> "He deserves pity who does not have an elder in his house." [23]

The elders represented the heads of lineages who were the more useful the older they became. One was told:

> "Face old age with confidence and not with fear,
> for old age is not tied to neglect or loneliness in Africa." [24]

Likewise, respect for elders is characteristic of black churches. Older ministers, church officers, and mothers' boards are held in high esteem. If not elected for life, deacons in Baptist churches and their counterparts in other churches are continually reelected and thus serve for life. Experience has taught that it usually takes more than three years to develop a man's instinct for "deaconing."

The practice of electing officers to life tenure, often beyond the period of positive production, was formed in West Africa, was in existence throughout the period of slavery in America, and still holds true today. Members, in fact, often expect young pastors to put older officers out to pasture, but it would be difficult to overcome a reputation for being inconsiderate to senior citizens. Full participation of senior citizens in the life of the church is essential to the success of a black minister.

View of Facilities

Church facilities are to be used by the membership and the community. Historically, the black church has been the city hall, community medical center, preschool, and public auditorium for the community. Because the church's facilities have in the main been limited to a sanctuary and basement, church school, youth meetings, choir rehearsal, and business meetings have generally been held in the sanctuary. The basement or lower level is often used for dinners or special programs. Far too many churches also put their children's classes in the church basement to "mold their character."

A small number of churches have erected educational buildings. If architecturally functional and if an effective director of Christian education is secured, the new facility is worth its weight in gold. Several pastors have, however, met opposition after the construction, for some teachers refuse to use the new building, feeling ill at ease in new surroundings, either because they were used to teaching between the pews, or because they discovered that they really had nothing to say and needed a high noise level to conceal that fact. A gym, too, could be used to great advantage if there were proper supervision.

Feelings About Training Clergy and Laity

Most black preachers function in direct relationship to their understanding of their call. The college-and/or seminary-trained pastor, fluent in black religious rhetoric and knowledgeable in black culture, is usually well received. Even senior citizens prefer the trained pastor who is prepared to meet the needs of young people of the present day. They've been heard to say, "I want a pastor who can read better than I can." The seminary graduate has not needed to boast of his training every Sunday or at any time, for the people remember that he is trained. His boasting could lessen his effectiveness.

While the aforesaid is often true, there is a feeling in some places that the trained clergy blocks inspiration and is a false teacher. Some of these people want the Bible interpreted just as "Jesus wrote it, from cover to cover."

> The well-trained minister is accepted if he can whip his followers into an emotional frenzy. He does not have to be a "whooper" but if he is good at whooping, he is the city's favorite. This is what is known as a versatile preacher that reaches the learned and the unlearned.[25]

Although the laity invests power to function in its behalf in the pastor and officers, the ultimate power in the church is actually in the hands of the church body. Of course, it has to be understood that any decision made by the body must reflect the will of the Holy Spirit. The Baptist principle that every election or vote is a poll of how people hear the Spirit disallows voting by personal preference of popularity. "Where two or three are gathered in my name, there am I . . ."(Matthew 18:20).

The laity is required to express itself for many reasons. First, "all of us are wiser than any of us." Secondly, the laity can detect latent ambitions in one another and when led by the Spirit, the right decisions will be made. Thirdly, those of the laity must be freed up to "scratch where they itch," so leadership will always know where they stand. The old preacher let everyone know exactly where he stood on every issue so that no one would stumble without light. Finally, the laity does inevitably express itself by voting "yes" or "no" on every issue. These votes are expressed by support or nonsupport of projects and programs. Again E. B. Hicks exhorts:

> We must train and utilize the laity in our churches and give them important things to do and then let them do it. The church will be far stronger when the pastor does not have to see to it that everything is done or does not have to do it himself.[26]

B. J. Perkins, a former treasurer of the National Baptist Convention, U.S.A., Inc., said, "You had better get somebody in the church with sense besides you. Look at a hog. You can toss a ten-dollar bill, a diamond, and a nail into the hog pen, and he'll root them all under because they have no value to him."[27] The layman should be prepared to serve in special positions. While the demand is not as great upon the laity, all through black church history, the masses of laymen have yearned for trained lay leadership. Needless to say, the black lay leader who had little training but desired to hold on felt otherwise.

Celebrations and Special Days

Among the Akan people of Ghana, celebrations and festivals occurred every twenty-one days. The Akan calendar was reckoned on the basis of nine festivals, bringing their year to full cycle. At these celebrations the chief "fed the ancestral stools," and the entire community rallied behind the chief as he performed the sacred rites.

Such celebrations provided opportunity for the elevation of the deeds of the chief and for regeneration of the society itself. Disputes of all types were settled after the stools had been fed. In this context, regeneration meant the reenforcement of social values and the strengthening of the solidarity of the community. Fun was a by-product of the festival.

On the occasion of the festival, part of the regenerative process was contained within many "praise speeches," which granted a recital of past glories and history, legends, proverbs, and the wisdom of the fathers, and provided the genesis of the oral tradition which even now obtains in the black church.

Laughter on these occasions grew out of appreciation, for much joy was expressed. The Akan people discovered the secret of maintaining harmony, joy, gratitude, solidarity, and genuine accomplishment within the family. Far too often Western culture looked askance at these festivals and relegated them to the limbo of a backward, aboriginal people in need of the "fruits of civilization."

The black church, following its African heritage, has raised a goodly portion of its finances through special days, which serve as vehicles of social benefit as well. The participation of members involved in the activities of special days is often executed in a dramatic way: men versus women, complete with general chairpersons and co-chairpersons, captains, committee members, and group members. A goal is voted, and often individual or group quotas are set. The real motivation comes, though, in the setting of the individual quota. What enthusiasm is generated! Nothing beats the individual participation of a maximum number of people on *their* days. Their activities serve as a model of social and communicative interaction worthy of in-depth research. The power patterns, the dress, and the self-images on parade are something to behold.

Anniversaries of churches and auxiliaries have been promoted as another means to raise money and to enjoy wholesome fellowship.

During church anniversaries and homecomings, many members return from all across the nation. They contribute financially and thus receive great recognition. The older the church, the more proud the members.

The churches which celebrate the pastor's anniversary often do so through the traditional pastoral reverence characteristic of many black churches, or out of a genuine respect for his leadership. It is a "give him his flowers while he lives" service.

Strengths and Weaknesses of Black Baptist Churches

Just as has every other institution, the black church has strengths and weaknesses, the delineation and development of which deserve an entire printed work. Here written, then, is what must be understood to be a brief summary of strengths and weaknesses.

Some Strengths of the Black Church

The black church:

1. Serves as a station of personal affirmation which attracts large numbers of persons;
2. Provides a rallying point for development of ideas on religion, politics, and all issues affecting immediate welfare;
3. Provides, because of its often limited personal and financial resources, a springboard for creativity through which those limited resources can be overcome;
4. Tends to impact greatly on the total community rather than just on its members;
5. Reposits the history, customs, traditions, and faith of black people;
6. Provides an arena for ongoing leadership development.

Some Weaknesses of the Black Church

The black church:

1. Often tends toward an anti-intellectualism which gives low priority to financial support of education;
2. Experiences daily confrontation with needs incommensurate with resources available;
3. Lacks, in too many instances, a trained and/or committed leadership;
4. Tends to nurture a sense of insecurity that disallows intra- and interdenominational cooperation;
5. Tends to rely on an oral rather than a written record of organization and administration.

While black Baptists have enjoyed a glorious history of support of missions in Africa, the Caribbean, and portions of Latin America, the overall support and total commitment to historic and emerging missions by Baptists has left much to be desired.

Black Baptists have not generally supported education in the local church or at the college or seminary level. A concept of total stewardship awaits further development in the black church. The socially imposed exigency of limited funds and its subsequent delimiting functional capability has developed in some congregations the tunnel vision that causes them to set priorities within their walls rather than without.

Black churches' funds have often been diverted to institutional maintenance (see chapter 7), away from education, missions, etc., to purchase and/or reduce indebtedness on facilities often deserted by whites in search of greener suburban pastures.

On the plus side, black church support of civil rights goals has constituted a legitimate "home missions" program. Many a civil rights organization would have closed shop if churches had not opened their doors, received free-will offerings, provided rent-free facilities, and offered general sustenance for survival.

Shades of the Black Church

Additional insights into black church strengths and weaknesses are revealed in a discussion on the "shades of the black church."

There are three cultural shades in the black church. The shades are Negro, Mulatto, and Black. However, 90 percent of the churches in the black community are *Negro,* irrespective of labels, such as Baptist, Methodist, Holiness, and the like. The Negro church is not integrationist although it has enjoyed periodic moments of fellowship. It may talk brotherhood, but its basic commitment is to its own.

The Negro church rejoices gladly and loudly and makes no apology for what it does because it is deep in the "black idiom and the big heat" and still has "wall to wall folks." As the late Louis Boddie of Chicago used to say, "I ain't got no sheepskin hanging on my study walls, but I got sheep standing around the walls."[28]

The Negro church, though basically conservative, has been an oasis of human love and understanding and will usually forgive any failure on the preacher's part except the failure to preach. Often called anti-intellectual, the Negro church is slowly changing as the third and fourth generations graduate from colleges and universities.

Not enough Negro churches have been involved in the struggle to unshackle the chains binding people. The Negro church, though afraid of the word "black," can become Black much more quickly than the Mulatto church.

The Mulatto church, contrary to belief, is not solely based on skin tones or shades of its members but on the adoption of white styles, white goals, and the imitation of white middle-class values and standards. Some Mulatto churches are "whiter" in behavior than some white churches.

To a degree, the Mulatto church has been integrationist. It is comprised of blacks in basically all-white denominations and "silk stocking" Baptist and Methodist congregations. Far too often, these churches have separated themselves from their poorer brothers while still attempting advocate roles through such groups as the NAACP or the Urban League. Unfortunately, some Mulatto congregations separate themselves from their less fortunate brethren and consider themselves a breed apart, only to discover in most instances that they are too dark to be white, yet too white to be black.

Mulatto churches, for instance, turn up their noses at gospel music because they do not wish to be identified with the singing of "cornfield ditties" and consider the anthem to be a mark of having arrived musically. While the Negro church has an acculturation problem, the Mulatto church has an identity problem. However, the Mulatto church that fails to adopt some semblance of black soul is in trouble, especially with its youth. The Mulatto church is generally blessed with capable, competent leaders in key positions in society who could, if ever they resolve their identity problem, help deliver liberation to the masses.

In an effort to keep pace with the time, some churches in the black community vacillate between the Negro, the Mulatto, and the emerging Black church, depending upon which choir is singing within a given church. There is a "Negro Sunday" when the gospel choir sings, a "Mulatto Sunday" when the Senior Choir mounts the loft, and a developing "Black Sunday" when the youth of young adult aggregations try to "put it all together."

The Black church is in revolutionary evolution. It will be a church demanding a clergy trained to an understanding and pride in its people, its history, and its faith, prepared to lead black people wherever truth requires. It will be a church eclectic, borrowing from all traditions and making them its own. It will be a church whose music will consist of stately anthems, gut-soul gospel songs, beautiful organ themes, persuasive pianos, bongos, drums, and guitars. It will be a church where celebration and festival, rejoicing and praising will be high on its agenda as it attempts to divest people of the "Gutenberg Syndrome" and put them in touch with their own humanity.

Since black is the mother of all colors, the Black church will be committed to all people. It will be universal and inclusive. It will be the church identified with the oppressed because the eternal God takes his seat among the disinherited. It will be the church surviving and living because it will welcome to its bosom all people who sit with the oppressed. The Black church is God's new creation.

Black churches, impacted upon by the civil rights thrust of the 1960s, reflect the subsequent changed self-identity of the black society and appear to be in the process of becoming *the* Black church.

The emerging Black church supports a value system with standards of excellence, which reflect black society's acceptance of its culture as a viable, meaningful, and productive way of life. It is a church evolving in black perspective. ". . . it doth not yet appear what we shall be . . ." (1 John 3:2).

3
The Pastor's Role in the Administration of the Total Program

To be a pastor is to be unlike anyone in any other profession or calling, for the minister, as he sees it, is chosen by God. "Ye have not chosen me, but I have chosen you, and ordained you, that ye should go and bring forth fruit, and that your fruit should remain..." (John 15:16), said Jesus to his disciples.

For many, pastoring is preaching, the delivery of thirty minutes of the gospel on Sunday morning. That's all there is to it; there is no more. For too many, the pastoral role is a soft job, a "pimping off the people" goodie.

On the other hand, many have taken off their blinders in order to see the ministry for what it is, a job so demanding that *no* person, common sense intact, would seek it of his or her own accord. God must do the calling, and the called must do the believing, knowing that God walks beside those who accept the call to overwork and underpay. Committed pastoring is a twenty-four-hour-a-day job.

Thus a look must be taken at those factors which impact upon a pastor's response to God's call, whether it be the first call to a pastorate or consideration of change to another.

What Should Inform One's Ministry?

Questions raised by a minister and family when the call to a church is contemplated are:

In what part of the nation is this church located?

How does the denomination, local/state/regional/national staff, feel about the ministry of this church?

What is the potential for growth?

What are the skills needed to develop the church's potential?

What is the history of the ministry of the church?

Who were the previous ministers?

What are the characteristics of their ministry?

Where are they now?

What support groups are needed to promote the full ministry of the church?

What community resources are available to support a full ministry?

What is the attitude of one's family about the change?

What is the quality of education available for the children, if there are any?

To what extent is the work to which the pastor is currently committed completed?

Do I honestly feel, after all this, that God wants me to go there?

What will be the cost of relocation? Who will assume costs?

What will be the salary? How does it compare with present salary?

In accepting a congregational call, a minister must be sure to light the candle and not curse the darkness. People must be met where they are. If they have lived on milk and crackers, his leadership cannot serve them solid foods immediately. Exercising procedural patience, the newly called minister, tempering all behaviors with consideration for what has been, must moderate and control the compelling temptation to change everything.

Academic preparation alone will not guarantee success, for the black church, though tending toward almost unanimous desire for a trained leader, may be suspicious of the seminary-trained upstart. The practices, traditions, and interpretations of a church deserve respect and must not be ridiculed no matter how worthy they may be of ridicule. After careful evaluation, group consideration, and patient nurturing, change comes.

Choosing the right people for the right job is essential to the success of any church. A minister must develop capability in selecting dedicated persons with training potential for a task and must allow them the mistakes that are concomitant to growth for as long as dedication remains.

Leaders must be chosen; leaders must be trained, for "it is better to put nine men to work than to do the work of nine men." This way is better even if the nine people do the job less than perfectly than the pastor could do it alone.

The Chinese philosopher Tao Teking, 600 B.C., wrote the following:

The best employer of men keeps himself below them;
This is called the virtue of not contending.
This is the ability of using men.
The great rulers—the people do not notice their existence
The lesser ones—they attack and praise them.
The still lesser ones—they fear them.
The still lesser ones—they despise them.
The leader is best, when his work is done, when his goal is achieved, the people will say, "we did this ourselves."

Teamwork is what capable administration is all about. A congregation working in apparent harmony with a pastor is the earmark of successful administration. An informed people, involved in the decision-making process at all levels, is basic to a successful pastorate. Without involvement, nothing lasting can take place.

The "merry-go-round" goes round; the schedule is too busy even to be called a schedule—it's an impaction—but the minister must never be too busy to take time with the people. The minister must be prepared to "tarry" a while. Persons have to be given sufficient time to feel that their minister has listened carefully to them.

A pastor must know well the members of the congregation; he must know the "churched" as well as the "unchurched" members of the family, the in-laws, the "out-laws," the children and grandchildren, the extended family. Getting to know all of the members of a family/clan/tribe/church is not easy, but failure to do so will work to the detriment of successful administration.

The minister with even a minimal penchant for success will attend all church business meetings with facts marshaled and, if necessary, documented; will be able to project self into the role of the fact recipient; and will never lead from behind.

A good administrator divides objectives into manageable parts and assigns them appropriately, anticipates problems, makes effective use of available leadership within the congregation, and never appears threatened even in the face of threat.

A good administrator excels in conflict resolution, faces it, turns disadvantage to advantage, and lets it be known that the "buck stops" with the pastor.

Open and above board in all dealings, the good administrator conducts affairs in such a manner as to make unquestionable the questioning of the pastor's integrity. Of course, sense common to the pastor is not necessarily common to congregants; so ideas will, understandably, be challenged and are subject to modification, but loyalty and trust will be forthcoming as a pastor proves worthy to receive it.

Essential, too, is discovery of a church's ebb and flow, the pace at which a congregation moves. Personalized pacing is characteristic of many churches and can be accelerated or decelerated once it is comprehended. To ignore the reality of personalized pacing is to court disaster.

Wise use of intellectual capability must be maintained at all costs. If a pastor accepts a charge that has rules and regulations that seem to "muzzle the ox that treads out the corn," wisdom dictates that he should wait until the propitious moment to bring about the needed change. Wisdom on the pastor's part also prescribes that any changes brought to fruition should benefit the church first and himself second.

Elliott Mason offers great insight into the leadership role of the black pastor by suggesting that those interested should closely observe a pastor at work. The powers of reflection, sensitivity to the congregation, and timing are most important. *How* the pastor functions may be more important than *what* he does.[1]

> When captain and crew understand
>   Each other to the core,
> It takes more than a gale
>   To put the ship ashore.
> For one will do what the other commands
>   Though both are chilled to the bone,
> And both together will sail through weather
>   That neither can weather alone.
> —Anonymous

A young pastor had high hopes for his congregation, but for some reason he had difficulty communicating with them. One of the deacons suggested that he have a talk with a veteran pastor of the community. The young man found the senior minister sitting on his porch one afternoon around 4 P.M. As the young pastor poured out his soul to the veteran "of the cross," it appeared as if the older man was not listening. The older man admitted that they had competition from the "switch engine" shuttling freight cars back and forth nearby. The young man said, "I have standards to maintain and the people must come up to where I am." The older pastor said to the young preacher, "Look at the engine, what is it doing?" "Backing up," the young man replied. "Now, what is it doing?" the older man continued. "It's hooking up to that long line of freight cars," the young pastor responded. "Now, what's happening?" the older man queried. "The engine is pulling the train forward," the young man replied. "That is exactly what you will have to do if you expect to pastor a church successfully," continued the senior minister.

There are pastors who will back up and remain in reverse. Still others will back up and hook on but remain where they are as they are. Every pastor must be willing to *back up, hook up,* and then *move out* from where they are to where they must go.

A pastor was accused of being a shepherd who did not bring sheep into the fold. To his critics he replied, "Sheep get sheep. The shepherd cares for, provides for, and protects the flock, but a shepherd cannot reproduce sheep."

"Shouldn't a pastor care for the sheep instead of shearing the sheep?" one sister queried. Then she continued, "All I ever hear in this church is money, money, money." "It is quite evident," the pastor replied, "that you don't know very much about the Bible or sheep raising. Jesus said more about money than he did about sin, salvation, heaven, and hell. He said that 'where your treasure is, there will be your heart also.' Furthermore," he continued, "if you care for the sheep, you will exercise good stewardship by shearing the sheep. The sheep grow a coat of wool that must be periodically sheared. If not, good wool will be wasted, for the older coat would be pushed off by the other. The quality of the wool is tied up in the shearing process." A good shepherd loves, cares for, and "shears" the sheep.

One needs to know what is expected and how well one is living up to role expectations. The fact that so much is expected of black pastors is not new. It goes back to early African roots in the extended family society. The following comparison is based upon criteria for evaluating the African chief's reign:

African Chief	Black Baptist Pastor
1. Fathers many children.	1. Presides at more infant dedications than funerals . . . signs of growth.
2. Succeeds in leadership, farming, hunting, negotiating for development.	2. Succeeds in building, fund raising, projects, etc.
3. Performs ancestral rites properly.	3. Preaches, pastors, administers, performs.
4. Administers traditional law fairly.	4. Administers the rules and regulations, written and unwritten, fairly. Shows no personal favoritism.

Where the above functions are executed, enstoolment is maintained. When these functions are not executed, destoolment is imminent! The parallel in the pastorate is impressive. One also needs to know how to read the folk appraisal, as illustrated here.

During the year that Deacon Johnson was chairman of the deacon board, and while the pastor was away on vacation, a clandestine meeting was held at which it was agreed to call the pastor into account when he returned from vacation, to confront him with some issues decided upon at the clandestine meeting, and if the pastor reacted in a certain way, to request his resignation. Deacon Johnson obeyed the directives of the clandestine group. On the other hand, he demonstrated his loyalty to the pastor by inviting the pastor to dinner on the Sunday before the requested meeting with the pastor was to be held, presenting the pastor with a beautiful new suit and a cash gift of $20. The pastor was puzzled by the gifts but accepted them. Later, after the meeting, at which Deacon Johnson attacked the pastor openly and with apparent great relish, the pastor understood the significance of the gifts, to wit: Deacon Johnson was saying to the pastor by the gifts, "I can't say no to my peers, so I am taking great pains to tell you I love you, and that you are to pay no attention to the things I do to you at the meeting that's coming." The pastor's reading of the situation was quite accurate. From then on he always knew when there was a disturbance or confrontation coming from his board. Deacon Johnson would begin three or four Sundays before a confrontational happening, giving the pastor little gifts of money. That way, he could say by his act, "I love you. Please forgive me for what I am about to do." These acts of gifts followed by confrontation continued for the whole of the pastor's ten years of ministry in the church. The amazing thing was, the pastor understood and accepted the apparent truncation in Deacon Johnson's attitudes and acts toward him (the pastor) and never saw Deacon Johnson, consciously or unconsciously, as other than one of his very best friends and most loyal members. When Deacon Johnson died, it was that pastor, who, although having been gone from the church more than three years, was specifically requested by the family (who had been so directed by Deacon Johnson) to give the eulogy at his funeral, and to have the very last words *(following,* not preceding, the Masons) at his graveside.[2]

Implementation

For good or ill, the pastor is basically the one who has the total picture/overview of the congregation, no matter how much responsibility is delegated to boards, committees, or individuals.

Worship and Care of Souls

A pastor makes or breaks his administrative role in the style in which he discharges his function as the leader of corporate celebration. His pulpit practice determines to a large extent the success or failure of his administrative role. In the pulpit, the pastor inspires, encourages, motivates, educates, innovates, lifts, and heals. Some call a real pastor a prophet, priest, promoter, pusher, and promulgator.

The pastor is obligated to plan worship services. While there must be room for the Spirit to move, the pastor should have an order of worship which is both intelligent and ordered, yet flexible enough to allow for the expression of the hearts of the people. The uninspired and uninspiring service sounds the death knell for the average black church.

The preacher is forced to "pastor from the pulpit." The minister must see that the proper instruments of worship are employed, be they one or several choirs, clapping hands, altar prayers, testimony upon occasion, congregational singing, instrumental music, or vocal response to what's happening. Feeding the intellectual as well as the emotional appetite, the minister's direction must be both cognitive and affective.

A highly trained layman once said, "I do not want a minister who will not make me cry sometime during the sermon and general worship service." "Make them cry this morning, Reverend," the older minister would say each Sunday morning to a young pastor. "If you don't make them cry, they will make you cry. It is better for one man to make a crowd cry than for a crowd to make one man cry."

To have made them cry means that the sermon was moving, challenging, and encouraging. Somewhere in the message a tender heartstring was touched which played the music of God's loving grace and hope for the future. When burdens are lifted, tears of joy overflow. It must be noted, though, that the spirited worship service may not necessarily be spiritual, and the stiff, dull service may not necessarily be intelligent.

The pastor must plan and conduct the worship to be both spiritually fulfilling and intellectually sound. Worship is essential for building the base for meaningful church administration. Some Orthodox church leaders from behind the Iron Curtain confessed at the World Council of Churches Assembly in Uppsala, Sweden, in

1968, that worship affirmed their personhood in the midst of dehumanizing situations. This has been the historic role of the black church and other churches. Those who would attempt to administer the program of the church must ever be aware of their awesome responsibility.

Christian Education

The pastor must dream more of growing persons than growing power or perquisites. He must also cultivate an atmosphere where dreaming can take place and where the people can participate in the dream vision. While the average lay person usually judges the pastor by the message of the sermon, true church growth must evolve from a sound program of Christian education.

Train, train, train! But the pastor must not err in considering himself the only instructor. A board of Christian education should be maintained so that there may be training for church membership and leadership. Making use of denominational staff, giving guidance in the choice of instructional materials, and making certain that the officers and teachers feel confident that the pastor is available for assistance are earmarks of the good administrator.

Finance and Business

Ideal is the situation where the pastor has little responsibility for the execution of plans regarding finance and proper business procedure. That ideal seldom becomes a reality in the black church. Where the pastor does not lead, there is seldom a financial program. The task is no easy one, for while leadership must absolutely come from the minister, that leadership must have the paradoxical attributes of being at one and the same time direct and oblique, for the leadership must be facilitating rather than authoritarian. Leadership must come from the pastor while appearing to come from the laity, for no financial program succeeds without the engendered cooperation and active involvement of the church membership. That's what administrative leadership is all about, leading the people into productive actualization, facilitating their doing.

The index of the success of any financial program is, of course, the actual filling of the coffers by the *many* rather than the few. Coffers filled, funds in hand, the prudent administrator assigns to a responsible and bonded board the counting and banking of monies, the paying of bills. To take on responsibility for signing checks or in any other way having direct contact with church monies is foolishly to pull down on one's head a crown of thorns.

This does not mean that the pastor, having given leadership to the management of a financial program, abdicates responsibility once the funds are in. In spite of the fact that the handling of finances is entrusted to persons of integrity and intelligence, their handling must be monitored via written reports to the pastor on weekly receipts, regular written reports to the congregation, dual systems of record keeping, and an audit by an accredited agency. The pastor must not retreat from pressing for the orderly administration of finances, because more confusion can be generated from the mishandling of finances than from any other aspect of church administration.

As the pastor leads in the raising of finances, consideration must be given to the three sequential steps to Christian stewardship:

1. Percentage giving—regularized giving of a definite percentage of income at a level less than 10 percent.
2. Tithing—the biblical concept of regularized giving of income at a level of 10 percent.
3. Proportionate giving—regularized giving of income at a level in excess of 10 percent and in proportion to what is considered one's blessings.

As perceived by the guide listed below, percentage giving is a steady progression up a ladder, each rung serving as a desensitization factor for movement to the next rung.

Weekly Income	3%	4%	5%	6%	7%	8%	10%
50.00	1.50	2.00	2.50	3.00	3.50	4.00	5.00
75.00	2.25	3.00	3.75	4.50	5.25	6.00	7.50
100.00	3.00	4.00	5.00	6.00	7.00	8.00	10.00
150.00	4.50	6.00	7.50	9.00	10.50	12.00	15.00
200.00	6.00	8.00	10.00	12.00	14.00	16.00	20.00
250.00	7.50	10.00	12.50	15.00	17.50	20.00	25.00
300.00	9.00	12.00	15.00	18.00	21.00	24.00	30.00

Tithing places one on the top rung of the giving ladder, representing the Old Testament admonition that God be given time, talent, and treasure (Genesis 28:22; Leviticus 27:30-32; Malachi 3:8-10; see also Matthew 23:23).

Proportionate giving is the extension of the giving ladder, and it represents a loftier elevation than tithing. It is a matter of severe personal scrutiny and conscience. Few there be, at this point in time, who go therein (Matthew 10:8; 1 Corinthians 16:2).

While some church members accept the concept of pledging, many others altogether reject pledging at any of the three steps of Christian stewardship. Pledging, though, is supported by the Scriptures: Psalms 50:14; 76:11; Ecclesiastes 5:4-5.

Tithing and proportionate giving hold the key to the survival of the black church. If, however, the church expects to elevate its membership to these levels of stewardship, according to Louis Smith, it must impact on those four environments that affect the lives of people:

1. The environment of work—where one earns one's daily bread.
2. The environment of school—where one is confronted by a meaningful educational process.
3. The environment of the street—where one finds peer acceptance.
4. The environment of religion—where one lays hold of the undergirding pillars of one's existence.[3]

Community Witness

It can be stated again and again that the black church is the largest single body in the black community which is organized for the good of the community. No other group can gather such numbers so often. Few black organizations can wield the influence that the church can. The pastor can reach more people on Sunday than many another can reach during a month of phoning and doorbelling.

Traditionally the black church has ministered to the whole person. As much as ever, the church must be in the world but not of the world. If the church does not speak, "then the rocks will cry out." The pastor, making use of social action committees and individuals placed in key positions of service, provides the community a platform from which "people united to save humanity" can be heard. There should not be a single area of community concern where the church is not making its weight felt. The church must address itself to every facet of life.

The pastor must be willing to share leadership in the role of community leader, for people desire participatory democracy and wish "to speak for themselves." The best way for a pastor/church to perform this function is in the role of an advocate—one who can speak or fight for another. Grass-roots people know their strengths and weaknesses. When they are in need of a strong voice or force, they seek the church. The church must respond. At the same time, the church must be wary of those forces in the community that would attempt to "rip-off, pimp-off" the church and never support it in any way.

Many clergypersons justify their participation in civil rights, community-action programs and business ventures as legitimate extensions of their ministries. Because the minister is often the only one in the community not dependent on "the man" or the "establishment" for support, his interests can be diversified and directed to many controversial issues without jeopardizing his job. Moreover, he is the one who can "rally" the people to a worthy project or cause. The black pastor is often responsible for securing jobs for many of his members and others in the community. Because he tends to have the respect of employment managers and other agencies, often a telephone call paves the way for employment. At other times, he may accompany the job seeker to the agency.

The same is the case with the Department of Welfare. Valuable is the pastor who will take the time to help those who need employment or welfare assistance, who will make that seeker of welfare, depressed by the seeking, feel that his or her plight has the pastor's full attention and sympathy. However small it may seem to the pastor, the problem is great to the seeker.

It should be stated here that the pastor who heeds the needs of his people will be approached by many outside his fold for assistance. He must serve wherever he can, going into all the world.

Often the black pastor is consulted on a matter of personal and family business. He must be very judicious and learn when to bow out and refer matters to others who are trained to handle the problem. He must not allow himself to be considered a specialist in all things—but a specialist in securing the resources to get things done.

There is the need to win the unchurched community to Christ. For this the pastor must train, train, train. House-to-house visitation is difficult and not too productive although some religious groups use this medium. And because the wise pastor takes the best of the old and the new in personal witness, he will seek people in those public places where many gather—laundromats and supermarkets. An enterprising minister has discovered a fruitful "visitation ministry" by spending a little time at the supermarkets where people shop on Fridays and Saturdays.

In this day of television, the attraction of sports, and the disparate working hours in even a single family, the church finds keen competition, which must be met with ingenuity. Offsetting that competition is the challenge of the church today and is probably being better met by the black church than any other.

Office Administration
Church Office Staff and Volunteers

Few black churches have an office staff of more than one full-time secretary. Where size demands and funds allow, the pastor should have an office secretary who can serve as administrative assistant. Even though secretaries are technically hired by the trustees, as executive officer of the church, the pastor should recommend to that body the secretary to be hired. Much follow-through can be effected by an administrative secretary without the conflict often caused by an assistant pastor, frequently nonsalaried.

In almost all black churches, there is use of volunteer personnel— not only because of lack of funds, but because service freely given is essential to Christian stewardship. Wise is the pastor who has the ability to choose good people and who trains them and puts them to work. Blessed is the church, too, that will especially utilize its greatest source of volunteers, namely, the youth and senior citizens.

Again, there must be an understanding of authority and responsibility. While others stress what can be done only by paid staff, black churches go ahead to do the job with volunteer help. Often, volunteer help does almost as well as a paid staff— sometimes better, especially on short-term projects. This is not to say that full-time paid staff is not better in some areas, but the black church would never get off the ground if it waited for the time when full-time paid help could be acquired.

Clergy Staff and Volunteers

Few black churches have more than one full-time clergy on the payroll because of the lack of funds. Moreover, it must be kept in mind that the black church, by and large, finds it difficult to function under more than one pastor. Black people tend to be unable to look at two leaders with apparent equal status within the same house, without becoming "cross-eyed." Only in a circus, and in the sideshow at that, will one find a "two-headed creature." Even with the finances available, the use of co-pastors will usually cause rough sailing.

The black church looks to *the* pastor to lead, guide, and direct. This is not to state that there cannot be clergy assistants, but it should be clearly understood that they are assistants-to-the-pastor, responsible to the pastor, and subject to the pastor's appointment and removal. Where such is not the case, there is always danger of confusion at the top. Frequently, members who desire confusion will tell an assistant that he should be the pastor. He is silly to believe them. The man whose salary the black congregation pays is the one they want for pastor.

Where the church has a staff of paid clergy in various capacities, the pastor should have the authority to assign responsibilities and to hire and fire. The same is the case with musicians. The officers can receive the pastor's recommendation and reach agreement with him on hiring, but the ultimate choice should be made by the pastor, because it is the pastor who has to work most closely with staff. The pastor should delegate authority and require accounting and stewardship, with a clear understanding regarding role definitions. Such can assure a harmonious relationship between pastor and assisting staff. They should not allow others to weaken their confidence in one another or their loyalty as teammates.

Consultants

In many areas of the business world, consultants have been used in great numbers in recent years. A church may not be able to hire full-time assistants, but enrichment comes in the utilization of the services of consultants whenever and wherever possible.

In fact, in building and financial programs, the expert is being called upon more and more. While a small minority still feels that God gives the pastor the answer to every aspect of the church's program, the wise pastor must realize that God can lead him to the expert in a particular field who is prepared to deal with the problem professionally. God works more effectively in many areas through the pastor's trained consultant. Wise is the pastor who knows how to shore up his own skills through the skills of others.

4
Principles of Structure

Some black churches seem reluctant to have constitutions and bylaws. Many that do are simply attempting to comply with the letter of the law which may be required in their state. Some churches claim, along with William A. Jones, Jr., that the New Testament is sufficient guide for them.[1]

"Whenever black people in church become legalistic, depending solely on constitutions, bylaws, Hiscox's *The New Directory for Baptist Churches, Robert's Rules of Order,* discipline, that institution," according to Elliott Mason, "is in serious trouble."[2] Power grabs are in the offing. Black people are basically a consensus-ad-hoc-oriented group. "While this statement is true, the situation becomes tragic when there is no Holy Spirit consensus, and there are no just rules of structure for a fair (though not holy) contest," says Henry Mitchell.[3]

The Need for Incorporation, Constitutions, and Bylaws

In these more complex times, it is mandatory that the black church, regardless of previous disinclination, deal with the importance of church articles and bylaws as an enabling vehicle in the achievement of its goals and as protection against internal and external encroachment on its rights. Any such church document must be legally and technically constructed, but it must also seek elevation beyond that which is solely legalistic and must express its legality in keeping with the humane and Christian guidance of the spirit of God as defined by Jesus Christ. Devised thusly, the black church concomitantly "destools" both the loose constructionist, that is, whatever is not expressly forbidden is permissible, and the strict constructionist, that is, the law must be followed regardless of the Word.

"A church reaches its maximum potential when informed by the Holy Spirit," states Kelly Miller Smith. "I believe in democracy," he further claims, "but there is a danger that people don't give credence to that strange, weird, mystical thing called the Holy Spirit."[4] Many church members tend to shy away from rules, regulations, and bylaws, for they feel they can become too frozen, static, and sacrosanct. Kelly Smith believes in principles as opposed to rules and regulations. Principles include primacy of faith, stewardship, and relationships to other people.

In today's world, churches should have articles of incorporation consonant with historic Baptist traditions. Churches should also be constituted with bylaws that are periodically reviewed. Admittedly, there is a danger that some persons will be "pharisaical" in their outlook and interpretation of the bylaws.

Thomas Elliott Huntley takes a position in his manual, adopted by the National Baptist Convention, U.S.A., Inc., as their standard doctrine in church administration, that

neither church nor pastor is entirely independent of each other; but are rather interdependent (like lock and key). The source of authority of certified constitutional processes, on this wise, are basically, unBaptistic unless they are effected upon the following conditions: 1. That such constitution and by-laws be written and approved with the mutual consent of both pastor and church only, and that no such constitution be written during a pastoral vacancy of said church; 2. that said constitution and by-laws be applied only to the administration and pastor by whom or under whom such was written; 3. that when said church becomes vacant, the pastor-elect be given 90 days to study the original constitution and by-laws with the privilege to revise or to reject the same, according to the vision that God has given to him for that particular field, or to reject that call if said church does not accept his vision; for "new wine must be placed in new bottles." 4. that no church hold a constitution and by-laws in abeyance, or in obscurity, for several months or years without the new pastor's knowledge, and then spring it forth as a secret weapon to obstruct his pastoral authority as the Holy Spirit has given unto him; 5. that the freedom of the pastor and church are not bound, monopolized nor dominated by any autocratic, or dictatorial unit, whether they be a deacon, a trustee, or any other executive branch that would destroy the freedom of speech and the Godly actions of the pastor and members—a freedom which is bequeathed unto them by the heritage of the Baptist fathers beginning with John the Baptist.[5]

Huntley presses his claim that

any constitutional provision differing from what he has stated is not in keeping with the doctrine of the Baptist Church. A Baptist church cannot operate exactly on the basis of an Association and Baptist Conventions (by constitutions and by-laws); for these are, largely shepherds' tents; whereas, the church is on the order of a sheep-fold led by the undershepherd of the Great Shepherd of the sheep where Christ is the center of influence and the law; and where the believers are no more under the law (legal documents) but under grace.[6]

Whatever the argument, black churches must have legal documents that direct their operation. Specifically, they must have articles of incorporation and bylaws. In fact, while the loose or strict interpretation of church constitutions might remain debatable, the matter of incorporation versus nonincorporation is a moot point, for the unincorporated church can be personally hazardous.

Unincorporated church officers or trustees are individually liable where civil cases and purchase of church property are concerned. Officers, having put up their homes as collateral when building a new church edifice, have lost those same homes when the congregation defaulted in payment. Under the unincorporated setup, the church property's legal title is in the hands of the trustees, with the congregation having no legal control.

Many states are forcing churches to incorporate in order to maintain tax-exempt status. This step has been a blessing both to officers who have carried individual burdens for the congregation and to the congregation itself who needed to control the action of trustees.

To state it again, churches should incorporate. This is a must.

Types of Church Corporation
Corporation Sole
This corporation is controlled by a single person. That individual or the successor in that role has full legal control which cannot be usurped by the congregation. This is the standard structure for a Roman Catholic diocese and bishop.

Trustee Corporations
Here the state grants power, through charter, to officers to act as trustees for the congregation. They may or may not be officers of the church or society. Once they are elected by the society, full control of the church property is in their hands. Even when the church buys, leases, or sells property, unless the articles of incorporation stipulate otherwise, the power to do so is already granted to the trustees. The only time the board is accountable is during annual meetings and elections. The trustees enjoy perpetual succession. When a vacancy occurs, the society may elect someone to fill the vacancy, or in some cases the trustees elect their own replacements.

Membership Corporations
The membership corporation is more easily understood. It is also

created by charter from the state, but the corporation here embraces the entire membership of the society. The distinction between trustees and society is eliminated, and there are but two entities, church and corporation. Its organization is similar to that of a civil or business corporation, the members of the society corresponding to stockholders, and its officers corresponding to the board of directors. Even where the officers are designated trustees, they hold no trust but are merely administrative officials subordinate to the congregation met in business meeting, to which they are answerable, and not to the courts.[7]

By and large, black Baptist churches are "membership corporations." E. T. Hiscox's *The New Directory for Baptist Churches*, which in some churches is the "law and the gospel," states that "trustees are really a standing committee."[8]

Varieties of Power Arrangement

Who has the final word in the black church? By what and whose authority does it move, operate, and function? The following charts indicate that a Baptist church is autonomous, sovereign, free, under the Eternal, to design its own destiny. The church is a spiritual entity.

A spiritual entity demands that the spirit have primacy over the temporal or mundane. A dichotomy between spiritual (deacons) and temporal (trustees) officers should never exist.

Chart A

Old Standard

HOLY SPIRIT

CONGREGATION

PASTOR

Deacons (Spiritual)	Trustees (Temporal)
nominations discipline	buildings contracts salaries program funds ("The Corporation")

Under the "Old Standard" arrangement, the congregation holds the power.

The pastor and deacons may make nominations, handle disciplinary problems, and take care of *spiritual* matters.

The trustees handle all business, *temporal* matters. They represent the church in legal matters.

Chart B

Old Traditional

(Unincorporated)

HOLY SPIRIT

CONGREGATION

PASTOR

DEACON BOARD
(de facto trustees)

Education	Fellowships	Worship	Business
Sunday school	men	choirs	
	women	ushers	

Under the "Old Traditional" arrangement, the church holds the power.

The deacons assume the functions of deacons and trustees by using a committee of the deacons to perform trustees' functions. There is a soundness to having one board, with or without incorporation. It avoids contests between boards. However, it concentrates too much power in one place. This isolates decisions from responsibility and constitutes a form of "taxation without representation."

Under the Joint Board arrangement, the joint board assumes the duties of deacons and trustees.

In Option 2, *deacons, deaconesses, and trustees* form the joint board. Such a threesome or more assures more harmony and more support for the action or recommendations of the joint board and allows the larger segment of church support, women, equal voice in giving direction.

The joint board may perform the legal functions or authorize the trustees to act.

Here again, the church holds the power, and the delegation of that power, together with all restrictions and accountabilities, is set forth in the bylaws.

Chart C

Joint Board System

HOLY SPIRIT

CONGREGATION

PASTOR

JOINT BOARD

---

budget   nominating

"OPTION 1"

HOLY SPIRIT

CONGREGATION

PASTOR

Trustees   Deacons

---

budget—nominating

"OPTION 2"

HOLY SPIRIT

CONGREGATION

PASTOR

JOINT BOARD

Deacons,   Deaconesses,   Trustees

---

budget—nominating

Chart D

Advisory Board or Council

HOLY SPIRIT

CONGREGATION

PASTOR

ADVISORY BOARD

Deacons' Board	Deaconesses' Board	Trustees' Board	Finance Committee or Board	Education Board	Missions Board or Committee
Parish Zones				adults	
			budget	men	
				women	
				young adults	
				youth	
				children	
				athletics	
nominating	ushers	music	publications	social fellowship	social action

Under the Advisory Board or Council, the congregation still holds the power, but the advisory board serves as a joint board which is more representative of all areas of the congregation. The result is that input from all major segments of program is heard before major decisions or recommendations are made. The working church does not face arbitrary actions from a remote lay hierarchy.

Chart E

Integrated Corporate Board

HOLY SPIRIT

CONGREGATION

PASTOR

CORPORATE BOARD

Deacons or portion of the board	Members of Trustee Committee	Clerk	President, Women's Society	President, Men	President, Ushers

or representatives

Under the Integrated Corporate Board, the congregation holds the power. The corporate board represents the church in legal matters.

An organizational flowchart with an explanation of the Antioch Baptist Church, Houston, Texas, follows for study:

ORGANIZATIONAL FLOWCHART

The organizational flowchart on the next page is designed to show in graphic detail the line of authority or, more appropriately, the lines of cooperation within our church.

It illustrates the manner in which organizations and boards are related.

It illustrates the position of the church in all matters.

The chart *does not* show Antioch as it is but rather Antioch as it might be if suggested programs are adopted and implemented.

The church is, however, obviously more than an organization even though it must operate by sound organizational principles. The church is, at its root, an organism which implies it has a *living* quality about it. The church must live through the people who compose it and through the witness of their lives.

It is clear that in the black Baptist church the congregation holds the power. The vote of the congregation is supreme.

The pastor presides, appoints, recommends, and directs with the consent of the people.

The people understand the pastor's mandate and call from God and will respect him in his role. When and if the pastor abuses his power, he is subject to removal. As in African tribes, the people will not "go over" the pastor, but they will "go around" the pastor. When necessary, they will "destool" the leader they "enstooled."

Black church officers and congregations must understand that it is both un-African and unchristian to create a dichotomy between spiritual officers (deacons) and temporal, nonspiritual officers or business persons (trustees). A church which fails to place "spiritually committed people" in charge of handling money will soon be in trouble.

ANTIOCH BAPTIST CHURCH *
ORGANIZATIONAL FLOWCHART

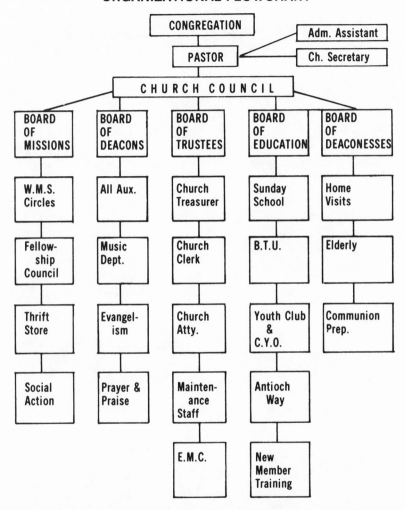

Jesus had a great deal to say about money and the use of money. "Where your treasure is, there will your heart be also (Matthew 6:21).

A good businessman out in the competitive world knows the value of the spiritual dimension. Says Lou Smith:

The spiritual/humanitarian dimension must have precedence over the economic dimension. Those who deal in the marketplace lose the spiritual

*This refers to the Antioch Baptist Church in Houston, Texas, The Reverend Doctor H. Beecher Hicks, pastor.

qualities because winning/losing, success/failure, profit/loss is the name of the game.

Economics are necessary, but a religious institution is in serious trouble if it permits the financial to dictate or control the spiritual. Utilize the expertise of the economic, but make it the servant of the spiritual, not its master.[9]

To be sure, there must be good business procedure in the black church. But where there is dedicated Christian commitment on the part of pastor and people, a fellowship develops which surmounts all obstacles, and the spiritual versus temporal struggle is changed to "Lord, what will you have me to do?" "Not my will but thine, O Lord."

5
Details of Administration

Clergypersons are now asking many questions about church structure prior to acceptance of a call, and they are making some conditions contingent upon their acceptance. It is only wise and fair that questions be raised in an atmosphere of openness and trust, for the black church is the only area over which black people hold fairly complete authority, and as such it requires the best management of its stewardship. Careful scrutiny should be given those areas where both church and pastor have deep concerns.

Questions Asked by Church and Prospective Pastor

Areas in which questions should be raised by churches regarding prospective pastors are:

Christian character
family status
education
age
credit rating
preaching ability
pastoral concerns
affiliations: religious, community, fraternal
professional history
philosophy of church organization, membership, training, church
    program, community concerns
role of the pastor's wife
counseling ability
evangelism
present salary; salary for which pastor is willing to accept call
references

Areas in which questions should be raised by pastors regarding prospective churches are:

number of active and inactive members
status of church membership list, i.e., updated or not?
residence of members
program of evangelism
view of pastor's role
view of officers' role
value of church property, insurance, benefits for unordained
church employees; Social Security, Workmen's Compensation,
medical and pension plan.
indebtedness
budget—categories
church incorporation? what type? bylaws? up-to-date?
church support of missions and education
denominational and ecumenical affiliations
spiritual climate
church's view of self as a family

Need to Establish Working Relationship

People have different backgrounds, dispositions, and training. For some, election to office changes their entire behavior. They assume the role which they feel the office requires. Thus, it may be dictatorial, authoritative, fussy, fatherly, or motherly.

The elected officer must realize that the church is a family where there must be compassion and consideration for each family member. While the officer may be responsible for a specific job, there cannot be the continual draining of a hard line of demarcation that states, in essence, "This is my job solely; that is yours."

That fatherly pastor has the wisdom to create a machinery that is conducive to the development of harmonious working relationships among officers. Often in the pastor's attempt to get officers to perform their tasks, nitpicking ensues. A pastor, promoting the image of the congregation as a family, cultivates harmony.

In many churches the natural leaders and prime movers may not hold leading offices but often move ahead in support of strong challenges which must be met by the congregation. The black church often finds itself launching a program which has come from the grass roots and ground swelling of auxiliaries who have tired of hesitation on the part of titular leaders. Interestingly enough, whereas the pastor hammers away not so much at who does *what* but at *how* the *what* is done, the officers and auxiliaries generally maintain the working relationship without which the "old ship" would experience rough sailing.

Church Officers

The black Baptist church has as chief officers the pastor, church clerk, treasurer, and financial clerk.

The pastor is elected for an indefinite term which ends either upon his decision or that of the congregation. Should there be termination of a pastoral relationship, severance is generally preceded by a notice of ninety days from either the congregation or the pastor. The pastor serves as moderator of the church unless otherwise decided. However, in some few situations a lay person may be elected as moderator and serve quite effectively.

The church clerk, elected annually, keeps all legal records, the minutes of all congregational meetings, an up-to-date membership roster, and writes letters of dismissal to other churches. The church clerk should be one who respects details, who has a sense of history and a regard for the careful recording of that history.

The treasurer, also elected annually, provides for the banking and disbursement of funds in keeping with the church's orders. No longer tolerated is the keeping of church funds in church vaults or the home of the treasurer, hence the greater use of Sunday or night deposits.

The financial secretary, another annually elected officer, keeps a record, along with the treasurer, of all funds received; keeps a record of each Sunday's offerings and deposits, each individual member's contributions; distributes church offering envelopes; and makes available an accurate statement of annual giving of each member. In addition, that officer maintains a record of the budget spending of various groups, gives them status reports so as to prevent excess expenditures, and makes an annual report to the church.

Boards of the Church
Diaconate—Deacons and Deaconesses

Deacons in black churches are usually ordained and elected for life. In some cases they are not ordained and are elected on a rotational basis. Each church must select the system best suited for its situation. Deacons are special assistants to the pastor, visiting the sick, serving as a disciplinary committee, overseeing the preparation of the ordinances of the church, that is, the Lord's Supper and baptism. Additionally, they attend to the problems of the needy.

In some churches, deacons count the church offerings, record receipts, and turn the money over to the finance committee.

Deaconesses are not ordained but are usually elected for life. In some cases they, too, are elected on the rotation basis. Again, the church must use the system best for its situation.

Deaconesses cooperate with deacons and the pastor in promoting the spiritual welfare of the church. They, too, visit the sick and shut-in and care for the needy. Additionally, they often prepare food for bereaved families and assume assigned tasks regarding baptismal candidates and preparation of the elements for the Lord's Supper.

In many churches, deacons and deaconesses have been given leadership roles in division of the church membership into zones or fellowship areas, geographical divisions of the membership which can operate as a church within a church. Certainly, this division leads to a neighborhood cohesion of members who might otherwise never have occasion to know one another. They amount, at their best, to small tribal or extended family units within the larger clan/family/ church.

In keeping with the recognition of the equal status of women in the church, some churches have placed women on the board of deacons, while others have made the deaconesses an official board to meet with deacons and trustees as a joint board. This last innovation promotes concordance and support for church programs.

The number of deacons and deaconesses elected depends upon the size of the congregation.

The Board of Trustees

Trustees are usually elected on a rotational basis. Some churches, however, elect the full board annually.

Trustees have the responsibility for maintaining and improving the church property, the handling of funds according to church budget and church authorization, and the buying and selling of property according to church authorization.

Usually there is a finance committee which counts the money. This may or may not be a committee from the board of trustees. The treasurer and financial clerk are usually members of this committee.

The trustees also provide for the proper security of church funds and an accounting firm to audit records.

A trustee board or committee thereof should be charged with the responsibility of studying the church budget throughout the entire year. Committees and boards which make use of the budget should have an opportunity to present their needs to the budget committee and should, in fact, have representatives on the committee. This would maximize participation in the budget-making process. By providing the members with the chance to make their input, the probability of reaching the proposed goal for the ensuing year is increased.

Persons should be trained to visit and enlist membership support for the budget proposal. There should be an annual financial canvass of the membership to underwrite the budget. Recognizing that the budget is not the ultimate fiscal word in the church, it behooves the leadership to plan carefully and to enlist support in order to attain a fiscal goal. Budget goals should be clear, evident, realistic, and reachable, for unreached goals create despair and a sense of futility.

Some people still have difficulty with the wisdom of a church having a budget. Far too many churches live from hand to mouth—by hope, chance, and annual rallies. The church of today cannot afford to operate on begging and impulse giving. Relatively predictable incomes should be paralleled by responsible and systematic stewardship.

Black church members have the privilege of pledging today because they are no longer dependent on the vagaries and fluctuations of an agricultural economy. When fearful, in the old pattern, of making pledges they can't keep, they forget the fact that God understands when a pledge has to be reduced or canceled. This is not true of their pledges for houses and cars.

The following serves as an example of what budget might be proposed:

SIMPLE SAMPLE BUDGET OF A MEDIUM-SIZE CHURCH

January 1–December 31

Current Expenses:
Salaries:

Pastor	$40,000.00
Church Secretary	16,000.00
Custodian	9,000.00
Assistant Custodian	600.00
Musicians	16,000.00
Bookkeeper/Treasurer/Financial Clerk	10,000.00
Church Gardeners	2,300.00
Security Officer	3,000.00
Parking Attendants	2,400.00
Parking Assistants	480.00
Neighborhood Watch	480.00
Culinary Department Manager	600.00
	$100,860.00

Operations:

Pastor's Auto Expenses on the Field	$ 3,600.00
Church Office Supplies	3,000.00

Church Envelopes & Bulletins	3,000.00	
Telephones	4,000.00	
Publicity	1,200.00	
		$ 14,800.00

Property Maintenance:

Supplies, Repairs, Services	$ 7,000.00	
Gas, Electricity, Water	7,000.00	
Pastor's Housing Allowance	14,400.00	
Insurances:		
Church & Workers Compensation	8,000.00	
Pension & Health Plans	10,000.00	
		$ 46,400.00

Organizations:

Board of Christian Education	$ 1,000.00	
Church School	3,500.00	
Baptist Youth Fellowship	1,000.00	
Vacation Bible School	1,000.00	
Boy & Girl Scouts	1,000.00	
Organized Athletics	2,400.00	
		$ 9,900.00

Miscellaneous:

Music & Choir Supplies	$ 1,000.00	
Decorations	1,200.00	
Convention Expenses	8,000.00	
Public Relations	4,000.00	
Social Activities	4,000.00	
Pulpit Supplies/Special Speakers	4,000.00	
		$ 22,200.00
TOTAL CURRENT EXPENSES BUDGET		$194,160.00

BENEVOLENCES

American Baptist Churches in the U.S.A.	$ 5,000.00
National Baptist Convention, USA, Inc.	5,000.00
Educational Institutions	5,000.00
Student Aid	5,000.00
Visitation Ministry	2,000.00
Special Ministries	2,000.00
Council of Churches/New Church Support	2,000.00
Assistance to needy & other local benevolences	20,000.00
TOTAL BENEVOLENCES	$46,000.00

Trustees should see to it that the church carries the maximum allowable insurance on its properties. Black churches are usually located in the inner cities and experience great difficulty in securing adequate coverage. Sympathetic agencies must be found or cultivated to provide protection for these properties.

Some church financial officers feel that to be bonded is to be considered untrustworthy. This, of course, need not be the case, for bonding is simple and wise insurance for both the institution and the officers. Bonding should be mandatory in all churches for those who handle and hold in sacred trust the financial resources of a congregation. An officer who refuses to be bonded should be refused the privilege of functioning as a financial officer.

All financial records should be audited not less than once a year by either an able auditing committee within the church or by a certified public accountant firm. Following this procedure will not only increase confidence in the officers but will also open the organization for record-keeping and administrative improvements.

The church should elect or select an attorney from within or without the membership to handle its legal affairs. If there is no committed attorney in the church membership, it might behoove a congregation to set up a scholarship fund for youths who will prepare themselves for the legal profession with the contracted understanding that they will, upon completion of their schooling, provide legal services to the church in exchange for that support.

Board of Christian Education

The board of Christian education, elected annually, has the task of supervising and administering the entire education program in the church. In the black church, this board has not really assumed its rightful place. It may become necessary for the pastor to appoint the members so that strong, qualified persons may serve. In almost every case, appointment, however made, must be followed by training.

The board is responsible for discovering, enlisting, training, and appointing all church education workers.

A strong board oversees the following: church school and its special day programs, vacation church school, supervision of the church nursery during the worship hour, Youth Fellowship. Youth Participation Day, Young Adults' and Senior Citizens' programs, training institutes, and retreats.

Advisory Board

Many churches have advisory boards composed of leaders from

every important segment of the church. This board may or may not take on duties of the joint boards, but it is advisable for reasons of increased communication and a broadened base of authority, wherever it is not rendered dysfunctional by misunderstandings based on culture.

When all areas of the church life are represented on a single board, the machinery is present for smooth operation.

General Details of Administration
Communication

Essential to the efficient operation of a church is an informed congregation. People tend to have confidence in the leader who properly gives notice of meetings, who sends informative letters, who issues reports—especially financial reports. If the pastor and official leadership do not inform a membership, someone else may misinform them. Although the pastor's sermon time must be for preaching almost 100 percent of the time, there are occasions when he needs to bring Bible teaching to bear on a specific crisis.

Letters to members, short and clear, will generate support far beyond expectations. While there may be criticism from a few, most members appreciate written correspondence from the pastor and the church. Some seldom receive mail other than bills; so a letter from the church is welcomed. Many members work on Sundays and, because of their lack of availability at other times, can be reached only by mail, making the use of a well-written letter an imperative. Caution must be taken that the letter not be confined to church meeting notices or finance.

Interestingly, usually when the black pastor is well accepted, the members do not attend business meetings well. When trouble brews, however, they come from all directions; thus, the church letter is important as a source of legitimate information.

Agendas

The church meeting, boards, and committee meetings should have an agenda which is used with tactful grace and intelligence. That is to say, use of an agenda trains the members and discourages unnecessary lengthy meetings. Many black churches have had business meetings run past midnight mostly because they were not properly planned. A pastor cannot cover every subject in one meeting. On the other hand, he must use his skills to work through the agenda without the impression of racing through or forcing decisions upon the members.

A suggested agenda for church business meetings is as follows:

Devotions
Minutes
Unfinished Business
Report of Church General Treasurer
Report of Church Benevolence Treasurer
Report of Financial Clerk
Recommendations of Joint Boards
New Business
Adjournment

The local church adjusts agendas to suit its particular case. An agenda enables the church to do business in an orderly fashion and to refer matters to the appropriate board or committee for proper consideration before coming before the congregation for a vote.

Accountability

Church officials should feel that they have an obligation to give a strict account to those who have placed them in positions of trust, for today's world demands accountability of those who would lead. Usually the matter of mishandled finances can cause the most trouble in the black church. Therefore, it is wise for church officers to make detailed and scrupulously accurate financial reports.

Meetings

More and more churches are conducting annual business meetings which include annual reports and the election of officers. During the year, an advisory council, comprised of the elected officers of the church and the heads of all boards, committees, and auxiliaries, or the joint board, consisting of deacons/deaconesses and trustees, meet to receive reports. When necessary, special church meetings are called to deal with specific items. Many churches, though, still conduct monthly and quarterly business meetings, but the attendance does not justify the effort or expedite the church's program.

A well-promoted and attended annual meeting guarantees adequate participation in the distribution of responsibility and power. Intervening meetings between the annual election and accountability of boards and committees are open invitations to the disruption of process. This is especially true when attendance is so often limited to a few faithful officers and a few disgruntled members, requiring low quorums if any official action is to be taken at all.

Whatever the meeting interval, boards perform the function of a clearing house to receive all items for the business session, build the agenda, and shape up the recommendations to be presented to the body for action.

Maximum Delegation of Responsibility

As many as possible must be found upon whom responsibility can be delegated. Because the black church has few paid and trained leaders, individual members must be given responsibility which might ordinarily be assigned to paid personnel. When put to work, they need not be followed every step of the way; but error must be expected at times. Such proliferation of responsibility, however, makes written reports mandatory. The bearing of responsibilities is the beginning of growth toward leadership and liberated self-determination both in and out of the church.

Denominational and Ecumenical Relations
Baptist Ministers' Conference/Fellowship

The Baptist ministers' conferences and fellowships are composed of pastors, associate pastors, and assistant pastors, and they represent a traditional body of ministerial camaraderie. For example, in the city of Los Angeles and vicinity, such a fellowship exceeds four hundred black ministers.

A pastor may become a member of a ministerial conference by virtue of the fact that he is pastor of a church in the area. An associate or assistant must have the sanction of his pastor to become a member. Dues are paid on a monthly or annual basis.

Such conferences and fellowships across the nation enable black Baptist pastors to improve themselves professionally; to support seminaries, colleges, YMCAs, civic organizations, and ministers in need; to become informed on community and civic problems and react as a body; to serve as an open forum for candidates for public office; to conduct institutes and seminars led by some of the nation's leading authorities in their fields; and to enjoy themselves in a great forum of preaching and lecturing.

In these conferences and fellowships, every member is somebody. That is to state that the organization recognizes all on an equal basis. Every type of preacher is heard as sermons are given each week on alphabetical rotation of names. Regardless of the size of one's congregation, the group gives the pastor who is a member of a conference a sense of being a part of a strong church body.

These Baptist conferences/fellowships consist of clergymen who are members of all of the leading national Baptist organizations:

the National Baptist Convention, U.S.A., Inc.; the National Baptist Convention of America; the Progressive National Baptist Convention; American Baptist Churches in the U.S.A.; and the Southern Baptist Convention.

Black Conventions

The leading black conventions in the nation are the National Baptist Convention, U.S.A., Inc., the National Baptist Convention of America, and the Progressive National Baptist Convention. Each has state convention affiliates.

Associations consist of churches in a small geographical area. The combined associations make up the state conventions, and the combined state conventions make up the national Convention.

By and large, churches give financial support, when the association meets quarterly, through representation fees for the pastor, the congregation, the women's missionary society, deaconesses, pastors' wives, church school, and youth groups. The local church brings its quarterly quota to the association meeting for the state convention.

The state convention has a mid-year session and an annual session. All pastors are members of the board of directors. The national bodies also have a mid-year and an annual session.

Churches are represented or pay fees to a national Convention on the basis of their numerical strength. These great black church Conventions are organized thusly: a Parent Body (pastors), Women's Auxiliary, Sunday School and Baptist Training Union Congress, Laymen's Auxiliary, Ushers' Auxiliary, Pastors' Wives, Youth Auxiliary, etc.

Such organization lends itself to maximum participation. Together, thousands of black churches support the same type of causes which white denominations support with regard to missions, evangelism, and Christian education.

The largest black church bodies in the nation are the Baptists. One-half of the black population is Baptist, to say nothing of the unrecorded Baptist leaning of those who have no church affiliation at all.

The history of national Conventions of the black church is glorious: their presence is influential and their future holds no limitation on potential.

American Baptist Churches in the U.S.A. and the Southern Baptist Convention

These two predominantly white church bodies, with more financial resources than black Conventions, are in a position to hire more personnel to implement their programs. Individual churches send monthly donations to the state or regional budget and the Convention budget. When a church joins the association or city society, that church is considered a part of the national body. Black Baptists are most proud of the institutions of learning which one of the mission groups of what is now the American Baptist Churches in the U.S.A. set up in the South during the Reconstruction Era. Many of the black leaders of our nation received their initial training in these colleges and universities.

Many black Baptist churches that belong to the National Baptist Convention, U.S.A., Inc.; the National Baptist Convention of America; or the Progressive National Baptist Convention, U.S.A. are now dually aligned with either the American Baptist Churches in the U.S.A. or the Southern Baptist Convention.

Reasons given by many black Baptist churches for dual alignment are: increased opportunities for interracial and intercultural relations, the attraction of retirement and health benefit programs, the possibility of loans for construction and improvement, educational programs and materials. In some instances, there are escapist churches who have joined all-white denominations, retreating from what they considered the worst of Negro Baptist Church/Convention folkways.

Since the emergence of the "Black Revolution" in the late 1960ş, many clergypersons and churches have taken a hard look at their reason for being in a basically all-white denomination. Many have defended the reasons already mentioned. Some feel they must "liberate white structures" from their inherent racism.

To the dismay of some white and "Negro" Baptists, most dually aligned black churches function in a "black style," even within the white structures. Black church people refuse to be coopted or dominated by white denominations and will function in the manner most comfortable for them. Mary O. Ross said, "There are no American Baptist churches in the National Baptist Convention, but there are plenty of National Baptist Churches in the American Baptist Convention."[1]

Dual alignment is frowned upon by many black church leaders. In some sections of the nation, dually aligned pastors are ostracized, and a few have lost status in the black state and national conventions. By and large, however, the resourcefulness of black people is soon recognized by those who have been critical when they see the obvious benefits.

City, Regional, and Ecumenical Bodies

The local pastor and congregation will be enriched by cooperative relationships and programs. Churches within a denomination and in several denominations can together tackle and accomplish infinitely more than one local church can accomplish alone. A pastor should, therefore, encourage both intra- and interdenominational participation.

As the official representative of the church, the pastor should keep the church in touch with all interchurch movements. Any pastor who limits his association with other organizations curtails the overall effectiveness of the church. In spite of this, members are often critical of their "much traveled" pastors, who must keep on the move to keep the church in touch with the world they are called upon to "save." The ministry of a local church can be greatly enriched through cooperation with others.

Cooperating pastors often open doors of fellowship and opportunities for an expanded witness for their churches. Cooperating pastors stabilize their congregations, find shelter in a time of "stress and storm," and develop supportive relationships.

The church must work with others to complete its mission; thus, conference participation and denominational and ecumenical affiliations must be encouraged. *No church is an island!*

6
Details of Program Structures of Ministry

The black church has opportunities to enter into several kinds of ministry in response to specific situations. There are the educational ministry, ministry to people through the celebration of the ordinances, crisis ministries, and wider ministry through service to the community.

Educational Ministries

Black church people tend to be middle-class oriented although many remain trapped in a low-income bracket. By and large, black church people encourage the education of their children, are frugal, strive to purchase homes and other property, seek job security and advancement, and invest in what they hope will be "meaningful church membership." Meaningful membership includes a viable educational program. There was a time when children followed their parents to church. Today, parents follow their children to the church—which demonstrates more than a pedestrian interest in young people. In fact, many parents will unite with a church shortly after their children's baptism.

Because the church's impact should literally begin "in the cradle," cradle-roll departments should be set up in which expectant parents, both members and nonmembers, are enrolled by the superintendent of the Sunday school. The pastor, notified of the baby's birth, should instruct parents in the obligations of infant dedication and should, thereupon, schedule the actual ceremony of dedication, further apprising parents of the age appropriate for actual church school attendance, and of the role of the parent at the time a child actually joins the church.

The prudent pastor does not underestimate the importance of an early contact with parents, for it wins parents as well as children.

A church, having secured and examined the educational tools and guides of its denomination, often supplements these through the use of materials from other denominations or independent publishers.

In addition to making use of denominational materials, some churches are now preparing their own literature for the educational program.

The heart and guts of the church's program are bound up in its educational trust. A board of Christian education is usually entrusted with the responsibility of promoting and giving leadership to this trust. Some churches have a board of education comprised of representatives of all areas of the church. Others spell out areas of concern, such as children, youth and adult work, athletics, missionary and stewardship education, and leadership training. The church school and fellowship groups, including the Baptist Training Union/Evening Fellowship, find shelter under the educational board's umbrella.

The diagram on the adjoining page was put into action with success in one local church.

The local councils of churches and some denominational staffs will be found ready to make available training for leaders who set out to make a local church program effective. Moreover, since cost may be a factor, the pastor and board of Christian education must be conversant with agencies who have the staff and resources to train local church workers.

Programs of Cub Scouts, Brownies, Boy Scouts, Youth Fellowships, church schools, and vacation church schools can operate well only under well-chosen and well-trained leadership. The pastor and board of Christian education have the responsibility to see that staff is trained. At times, the volunteers must be transported to the institutes and schools. At other times, the instructor may come to the local church to conduct the studies with the staff.

Very cogent concerns about the black church are called to our attention by Joseph R. Washington, Jr.

> Knowledge or the love of learning is not the only power, it is the *ultimate* power in religion as in every other dimension. Critical knowledge of world religion and church history, thorough study of theology and the Bible, and, finally, rigorous thinking are minimal but essential means to keep a church alive and therefore respected. Such a church will be irresistible to rebellious youth and confused adults.
>
> This is what the black church has to learn for itself. The love of learning has not been tried and found wanting; it has not been tried.[1]

Ordinances and Sacramental Ministries
Baptism and Training for Membership

In the Baptist church body, there are only two ordinances, baptism

BOARD OF EDUCATION

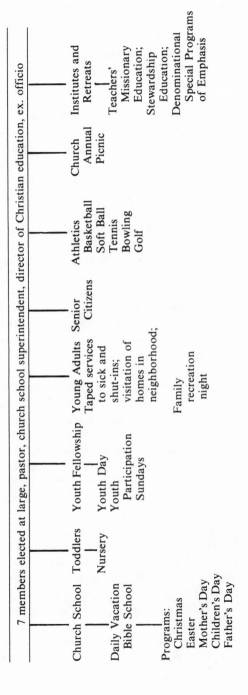

7 members elected at large, pastor, church school superintendent, director of Christian education, ex. officio

Church School

Toddlers
Nursery

Daily Vacation
Bible School

Programs:
Christmas
Easter
Mother's Day
Children's Day
Father's Day

Youth Fellowship

Youth Day
Youth
Participation
Sundays

Young Adults

Taped services
to sick and
shut-ins;
visitation of
homes in
neighborhood;

Family
recreation
night

Senior Citizens

Athletics

Basketball
Soft Ball
Tennis
Bowling
Golf

Church Annual Picnic

Institutes and Retreats

Teachers'
Missionary
Education;
Stewardship
Education;
Denominational
Special Programs
of Emphasis

and the Lord's Supper, or Communion. The pastor or director of Christian education, if there is one, should conduct classes in training for church membership. The classes are generally made up of youths from the church school and are usually conducted on Saturdays. If the pastor conducts the classes during the Lenten period leading up to baptism at Easter time, he may need to use the church school period for instructing the young people.

Since it is generally not effective to have children and adults in the same class, adults should be instructed separately. Denominational bookstores have materials which are appropriate for each age group.

Almost all black churches extend the invitation to membership during the worship service after the sermon. Classes in training for church membership may follow. At the Communion service, the newly baptized candidates and those who have united by other means (a letter from a sister church, a statement of Christian experience, restoration) receive the "right hand of fellowship" before receiving the Lord's Supper. This rite symbolizes full acceptance into the voting membership and is usually given by the diaconate as well as the pastor.

Baptism is a public initiation service where the candidate, through the act, declares a personal stand for Christ. Baptism is symbolic of the death and resurrection of Christ, with baptism by immersion representing Christ's burial and the rising out of the water, the resurrection.

The baptismal service should be solemn, personal, and meaningful and should be carried forth with dignity and in a spirit of creative celebration. In the service, the candidate's name should be called clearly and loudly, because it celebrates identity, and family and friends take pride in the act of baptism. Moreover, the baptismal service should be a part of the regular service. While midweek may be convenient for the pastor, the impression may be left that baptism is not important, because many will not or cannot witness midweek baptism.

Deacons and deaconesses must be well instructed as to their duties in caring for candidates for baptism. The deacons are responsible for filling the baptismal pool (baptistry) with warm water and for the preparation of verified lists to preclude youths presenting themselves for baptism merely because their friends are candidates and they want to get through baptism before uniting with the church. One deacon may assist the pastor in the pastor's dress preparation for the baptismal service and in the action of immersing the candidates. These traditional tasks have solemn meaning for black deacons.

The deaconesses attend the female candidates and see that all baptismal garments are maintained. They also instruct female candidates relative to personal clothing required during and after baptism.

Communion

The Communion bread and wine, sometimes grape juice, are prepared either by deacons or deaconesses, according to the local church's practices. Unleavened bread may be purchased from denominational agencies, although it is sometimes prepared by a team of deaconesses. Individual glasses and trays for the wine are used by most churches. The deacons serve the congregation at the direction of the pastor. The deaconesses wash the glasses and trays and place them in the cabinet set aside for that purpose until the next Communion.

Deacons dress uniformly, usually in dark suits with white shirts and dark ties, and they often serve Communion with white gloves. Deaconesses usually wear white dresses, uniformity making for an impressive service. It can be said, however, that Baptists believe that the spiritual condition of the person is what is most important, for dress has no saving power.

Organization and practice by the pastor and deacons will enable them to serve Communion with dispatch. The size of the congregation should present no problem to prepared deacons and deaconesses. The satisfaction of doing their solemn task well is one of their chief joys and a manifestation of their importance as persons.

The Lord's Supper should be administered when it is conducive to maximum participation. Where most of the congregation returns at the evening hour, it can be held at that special time. However, in the present urban experiences of mugging and break-ins, many members are afraid to return to church at eventide, so more and more churches serve Communion at the regular morning worship. Even in those churches where the main Communion is conducted in the evening, accommodations are made for those who simply cannot return by serving them Communion in a chapel or a section in the sanctuary set aside at the close of the morning service. Here again, the pastor and officers must consider the needs of the congregation.

Special requests for serving Communion to the sick and shut-in must be met. However, the practice of serving all the sick and shut-ins may be impossible for the pastor alone. If the diaconate will assume the task, it may work. They should not begin unless determined to continue. Once the practice of serving Communion to the sick and shut-ins is started, it is expected that it will continue. Deacons and deaconesses should be thoroughly instructed on administering to sick and shut-ins.

Marriage, Premarital Counseling, and Weddings

The minister should have a program of premarital counseling and should endeavor to hold at least one session of counseling with the couple prior to the making of extensive wedding preparations. Moreover, he should advise them to consult with their physician on many questions. The minister may secure counseling materials from his denomination and should attend institutes and seminars on premarital counseling.

Regarding the wedding ceremony, where possible, someone other than the pastor should direct rehearsals, with the pastor communicating any special instructions to the director. The pastor's directives should be given during the counseling, and the pastor should go through the ceremony with the couple to make sure they really understand it. His admonitions should be given in counseling sessions, not before the congregation during the ceremony. Here again, the minister is responsible for projecting the solemnity of the service and impressing upon the wedding assemblage the importance of such an occasion.

Crisis Ministries
Care of the Sick, the Indigent, and Confined

Where possible, the pastor must visit the sick. There is no substitute for his visit, for sick members want to see the pastor, want to experience his prayer. If he cannot go, it may be possible to reach the sick by telephone and use that as a vehicle for pastoral prayer. In the large, sprawling city, prayer by telephone can be quite effective.

The sick visit should be short, but the pastor should not appear to be in a hurry. Doctors advise brief visits of not more than three to five minutes. Where it is utterly impossible for the pastor to cover the field of the hospitalized and sick-at-home members, a minister of visitation could be very helpful.

In addition, the deacons and deaconesses should supplement pastoral efforts by systematically visiting the sick and shut-in and making reports therefrom to the pastor, especially if there is a need for financial assistance. Here again, the pastor must instruct his visitors of the sick, for they cannot be expected to lift the spirits of the sick without appropriate instruction. They must understand that a sick visit is not a gossip session, not a time to criticize some program or leader, not a time to talk about the visitor's operations or ailments nor his relatives' ailments, not a time to tell of others who are ill, have the same ailment, or have just passed on. Pastors should train all hospital visitors.

The sick visit is not a time to sing loud songs, preach sermons, or pray loud prayers. The visitor of the sick is to be instructed to get in, try to be uplifting, and depart!

Furthermore, the visitor has no authority to tell others what the ailment is. Let the patient, family, or doctor give that information. Thoughtless is the pastor, too, who announces from the pulpit the particular ailment of a sick member.

The pastor should provide materials for the sick and shut-in to read, or a committee of members may be formed to take the taped Sunday worship services to the shut-in.

Deaths and Funerals

Death is no stranger in the black community. There is no more important time to the family for the minister to be helpful than at the time of bereavement. Wise is the pastor who learns to serve the bereaved with sensitivity. The pastor should grant the wishes of the family where possible and should not create problems with some strict rule which places a still greater burden upon those in sorrow. A telegram, representing the concern of the entire church, may be sent to the families of the deceased whether in or out of town.

Because bereaved families are seldom able to understand the full implication of loss, the time of death must be considered inappropriate for instruction or object lessons. Getting to the home of the person responsible for funeral preparations as soon as possible, the pastor must seek to expedite the logistics thereof with as little confusion as possible, perhaps using a small committee of family and friends to prepare the order of service for the funeral, write the obituary, and facilitate the flow of preparations.

Often, the deaconesses' board or a similar group prepares food for the family. In the matter of death, the pastor must again instruct the officers and others on what to do and what not to do. Officers should not go to the home and hold prayer meetings with songs and prayers, one person trying to outpray the other. Such action simply adds to the sorrow of the family. Where a member of the family is ill, such excitement increases the illness.

And certainly the pastor himself is not to indulge in loud singing and praying and the deliberate delivery of a tear-jerking eulogy. His conduct should exhibit good judgment. His message at the funeral, indeed, the selections of the choir/or soloist, should be brief and comforting, all being used to bring calm and solace to an overwrought and burdened family. In addition, the funeral service is not the time for the minister or anyone else participating in the service to "candidate" or star. All participants must submerge self for the good of the family.

There is a growing trend to have a brief graveside-committal service for the family of the deceased and a memorial service at a later time.

Where lodges participate in the funeral service, the pastor should not show signs of disapproval, if he does indeed disapprove. He should do his part well and be attentive to the lodge service. If the family wishes lodge participation, the family's wishes should be granted to the extent that they are not in conflict with the church's funeral policy.

Black people are an emotional people. It becomes the responsibility of the black pastor, therefore, to help the bereaved to channel their grief creatively and constructively, but no black pastor can afford to frown on the strength of black culture in facing death (including viewing the remains) and doing healthy "grief work."

Delinquency and Adult Arrest

The black pastor should know the elected officials and power brokers of his city and state. He should also be sensitive to the community feelings about police relations, at the same time maintaining his integrity and creating a channel by which he can be of great assistance to his people. Quite often youths and adults are paroled to the minister for supervision. The black pastor has more than his share of this participation, but he recognizes that he has no alternative to advocacy and assistance for a people often unjustly caught in the toils of the law.

Prison Ministries

If you wonder where all the young men have gone, just visit the average correctional institution in any given environ and you'll find them. Alvin Poussaint believes the Black youth between eighteen and thirty feel they must strike out physically at a repressive society. Hence, many of them either die young or are incarcerated in a penal facility. The church must address this problem. Often the city has a prison chaplain who is quite cooperative with the pastor regarding those who need or request his services. The pastor should make use of the chaplain's aid.

Moreover, churches should be willing to lead worship services in prison. The pastor is often called upon to visit the prison. Here again, he must respond and be at his best.

It should be stated here, too, that those in prison appreciate correspondence. The pastor and a special committee should keep the mail flowing. Prisoners are encouraged by a letter. Even a church bulletin lifts their spirits. Many a prisoner receives mail only from his church. Keep it flowing!

Armed Forces Personnel

Every effort should be exerted by black churches to keep in touch with its members serving in the armed forces of the nation. Churches located near military bases should establish working relations with the personnel, especially with chaplains.

Many blacks reenlisted for additional military service immediately following World War II and the Korean conflict and served for twenty or more years. As a result, many have retired while relatively young and provide for some churches an ample resource of lay leadership.

Contact maintained with armed forces personnel, especially while they are stationed at posts far from home, helps to cement positive relationships and attitudes with the church. Letters are important in doing this.

Expanding Areas of Ministry

Everyone should not be expected to fill traditional church offices, such as deacon, trustee, choir member, usher, or church school worker. The church must, however, put to work the vast variety of skills and expertise residual in the laity. The laity is blessed with so many skills today that it behooves a sensitive congregation to build a "skills bank" so that all the members can be involved in meaningful activities. Wisdom has proved that young pastors should surround themselves with "seasoned officers" while at the same time opening up tight or closed boards so the infusion of fresh air and new blood may take place. What are some of the opportunities beyond the traditional?

Nonprofit Housing Corporations

Since most black churches are located within the inner cities of most major cities, and since most inner cities are permitted to decay by design, black churches should reverse negative trends by taking advantage of low-cost government housing programs and rebuilding the inner cities. Senior citizens, single young adults, and many families with children do not wish to depart from their "turf."

Day-Care Centers

Many pastors and churches have established day-care centers which not only give wholesome training to children, but also free parents for work or other services. Usually, the fees paid by parents or other agencies cover the cost of staff and operation. Government agencies and foundations have encouraged day-care center growth and sometimes subsidize programs. The present- and future-oriented church should conduct a feasibility study to determine the need for day care and the church's capacity to meet the needs. The staff must be hired. Because it is never advisable that the minister administer the center, a director must be sought who, along with the staff, must be efficient enough to prevent placing additional burdens upon the pastor. Upon graduation from the church day-care school, the children should be equipped to meet the educational challenge found in public, private, or parochial schools.

Credit Unions

Every black church with five hundred or more members should organize a credit union. Churches with fewer than five hundred members should link themselves together to offer to their congregants economic alternatives. A credit union is one of the best examples of "applied Christianity," for it facilitates the ego-raising dignity of a good credit rating. Credit unions enable people to consolidate bills, educate their children, make home improvements, support the "special needs" of the church, and meet other goals.

Cooperatives

Leon H. Sullivan's Zion Baptist Church of Philadelphia, Pennsylvania, demonstrated what a black church could do by marshaling its economic resources. The "10-36 Plan" was born when the Reverend Sullivan asked the members who would be willing to invest $10 per month for thirty-six months to remain after church. Two hundred people signed up as investors.

One day a young couple confronted Leon Sullivan with the fact of discrimination they encountered when attempting to rent an apartment. The Zion Associates Corporation, the cooperative launched by the "10-36 Plan," bought the apartment house and mandated "open occupancy." This is the direction in which black churches must move.[2]

Investments

Furthermore, black churches are discovering the new and profitable world of investments. At one time it was considered wrong to speculate with the "Lord's money" on the stock market. Today, it is considered an act of wise stewardship for churches to invest their resources in treasury notes, stocks, bonds, and mutual funds. Faithfulness in little things is now subjected to new interpretations.

Radio, Television, and Cable Ministries

No sooner do churches wake up to opportunities extant in the communications industry than there are more doors to walk through than there are people to take the walk. Radio still reaches many people. Many black churches broadcast their worship services, and a few have broken into television. Cable television is in its infancy and it presents to the church a chance to get its message across in an almost unbelievable manner. A church on the cutting edge must not let the "harvest" of this opportunity pass.

Church as the Hub of Community Organization

The church must be in the heart of the community and the community must be in the heart of the church. The church must, if need be, "lay down its life for the community." However, if the church is to be sacrificed, it has to make the choice of which "cross it will be crucified upon." The church must loom large in any community organization which exercises power on its turf.

Delivery of health services presents the church with opportunities to use its facilities to provide its constituents and community with the full range of medical, dental, and psychological benefits needed in a fast-paced society.

While the church must open its doors to serve people, it must be selective as to whom it will let use its facilities. A church should develop guidelines spelling out in no uncertain terms how its facilities will be used, at the same time making clear its commitment to relevant ministry.

Some churches have this motto: "We enter to worship; we depart to serve." Both can take place today only with effective administrative structures and with training for worship and for varieties of service.

7

Church Relocation, Renovation, Architecture, and Construction

... ownership of land is a basis for civic and economic power. ...
The matter of land and the relationship of Black people to land has considerable significance both for the social health of general society and also for the Black community's own welfare.[1]

One way for a disinherited racial group in America to move into the mainstream is to acquire land. The above quotations, from a Rockefeller Brothers' Fund report pertaining to the decline of black-owned land in the rural south, have serious implications for black people in cities as well!

A landless people lacks a base for future growth and development. The fact that some 75 percent of our U.S. population is crowded onto less than 27 percent of the land should spur black churches to acquire as much land as possible both in urban and rural areas North, South, East, and West. Acquisition of land by churches must, of necessity, receive top priority on the survival agenda of black people.

Black church ownership of a part of "mother earth" can provide a land base for the black community. The majority of black churches in most American communities are located in the areas reasonably close to the downtown business districts in the areas where black people have been living.

Now an increasing number of blacks are facing the prospect of impalement on the horns of a dilemma. The dilemma is that of having to choose between fleeing the ghetto for the "better neighborhood" and remaining in the traditional community where real-estate values will eventually increase.

Loans for rehabilitation of older areas have been nil. However, whites are buying all the inner-city properties they can amass. Why? Ghetto land is valuable, and long-range agendas abound to remove blacks and replace them with tax-paying whites in small office complexes, condominiums, and apartments featuring close-in working and living.

True as it is that the urban unrest of the 1960s hastened the demise of many inner-city communities, there is strong feeling that numerous "riots" were the creation of the "business interests" of the affected cities.

The two basic tactics for dislodging blacks from their "turf" are urban renewal (Negro removal) and highway construction. These two schemes have been both a bane and blessing to black churches, resulting in the need to secure and renovate existing church edifices or to erect "more stately mansions."

This chapter undertakes the awesome task of establishing the basis on which churches relocate by acquiring other properties or constructing new religious facilities. The areas for consideration in this chapter will include financing church relocation/renovation/construction and the use of architectural service, plus special problems involved in utilizing the skills of nonwhite contractors, subcontractors, and workers.

Establishing the Need

Recognizing the necessity of establishing a land base for black people, black churches should be constantly alert to every opportunity to secure land. Churches should, however, scrutinize their motives for purchasing land and/or securing other facilities. Some motives for church property acquisition are worthy, and some are not.

An "edifice" complex and competition are to be avoided. A charge has been leveled at religious institutions that they have wasted too much time and too many resources constructing churches to satisfy ego needs of the pastor or the congregation. Buildings should be built for people and not people for buildings. Physical structures should be created to meet the *needs* of a congregation.

Competition with sister churches has forced some congregations into building programs before real needs have been ascertained. The need to build should be realistically determined before launching a capital improvement program.

A congregation should exhaust every possible avenue of securing input from many sources to arrive at a decision concerning its future. After a season of consciousness raising, the first step should be the election/selection of a representative committee empowered to collect data and report it to the church membership. Without membership input and support, no major effort will get off the ground.

Population trends, surveys, and projections of future use by the surrounding area, proposed road improvements, and proposed zoning changes should be collected by the committee. Coupled with this data should be input received from the church membership, residents, and community entrepreneurs. From this material, a picture will emerge about the future of the area.

Sometimes a congregation desiring to serve its constituency and community more effectively in the present and for years to come will utilize the services of its denomination or an appropriate local university department to conduct a community survey of conditions, trends, problems, needs, and projections. To commence a capital improvement program without gathering pertinent data is like going to sea without a compass.

As a rule, people do not make decisions or changes unless forced to do so. Churches are no different. Congregations will clean up, paint, repair, and renovate facilities because of pride. Rarely do churches consider building unless they are confronted with urban renewal, institutional expansion, highway construction, or dilapidated facilities beyond repair.

Financing

It would be ludicrous to entertain the idea of land purchase or church construction without a plan to secure adequate funds (see Luke 14:28-30).

A congregation should plan the work of financing its venture and then work out its plan. If the need for capital improvement has been determined, then the church should utilize its planning committee or create one with credibility in the membership.

Recommendations from this special committee to the church should specify that: there will be a Building Fund (if one does not already exist); funds earmarked for Building Fund will be used for no other purpose; and accurate records of receipts and disbursements will be maintained for at least a five-year period preceding actual construction.

Adequate planning for basic financing of the intended project will serve to instill confidence in the membership to support a fund-raising effort and will develop a sound track record of accomplishments aimed at making financial institutions amenable to requests for loans.

Fund Raising

From time immemorial people have been most innovative in the area of raising funds to achieve desired ends. Capital-improvement funds generally must be secured above and beyond the regular areas of church contributions, namely, current expense and benevolence. Far too many church members, when confronted with a new worthy appeal, will either go overboard in their support of the new, or they will neglect that which they are already committed to support.

Nest Egg

Very few black churches which have not received funds from the sale of properties due to either urban renewal or highway construction are engaged in capital improvements. Many a building effort has sat on dead center until some major "community improvement" agency with the right of eminent domain made the church an offer it could not refuse.

"Nest-Egg Funds" can be a blessing to a religious body. The following are fund-raising methods that encourage *total* support of the church.

Systematic Giving

Members contribute their gifts on a regular weekly (not weakly), biweekly, or monthly basis through the use of envelopes. These funds are used for the sustenance of current expenses, benevolences, and the building fund.

Tithing Plus

This plan is systematic giving at a rate of 10 percent or more of a person's total income for church support. The funds so given are apportioned as directed.

Remembrances, Memorials, Wills

Remembrances are gifts donated in honor of one still living. Memorials are gifts donated in memory of one deceased. Wills make possible gifts to the church or to one's favorite charity after one's death, as directed by the person before his or her death.

Special Efforts

Capital Funds Campaigns are led by a professional fund raiser who works with the church to establish goals and to solicit the membership for pledges made to be fulfilled over a three-year period. Because a few professional fund-raising companies have had adequate opportunities to raise funds in black institutions, many are still in the process of developing skills and personnel that have relevance to blacks. They should not, however, be overlooked, for their methodology can be modified to make significant impact upon the black church.

Special drives or rallies may be conducted to solicit support for goals determined by the membership. These funds, as well as those secured via offerings and gifts, should be invested wisely prior to construction.

Building Funds Investment

Savings Plans

Regular full service banks offer the lowest interest rates of about 5¼ percent. These institutions provide opportunities to secure higher yielding bank notes.

Savings and loan companies offer better interest rates than full service banks.

Denominational saving plans offer specific interest rates contingent upon the amount of time funds are committed to the program.

Investments

Unthinkable for black churches in the past, investment plans are now acceptable. At one time, black church members considered the "speculation of the Lord's money" sinful. Experience gained through participation in the "war on poverty" and other perception-expanding ventures has increased some black conceptualization of Christian stewardship. As a result, other types of investments are being weighed by black churches, such as treasury notes, stocks, bonds, and mutual funds.

Treasury notes purchased at a cost of $10,000 each, yielding 9+ percent interest, are perhaps one of the fastest ways to make funds multiply. Early investments in treasury notes can benefit the church far beyond imagining. Stocks, bonds, and mutual funds present churches with other long-range possibilities for creating new capital. The average church member is not equipped to "play the market," but untapped potential exists for the corporate church.

Bonding Programs

In some parts of the nation, bonding programs have been popular for capital improvement and fund raising. To initiate this program, a church should float bonds through a bank, insurance company, or bonding agency, and sell them to the membership, to be redeemed in a specified number of years, yielding a guaranteed percent of interest.

The advantages of the bonding program are that a church can realize its dream of a new facility immediately if the bonds sell. A disadvantage of the bonding program is that the bonds are redeemed first. For example, if the bonds are redeemed each week at $500 per Sunday and on a given Lord's Day only $625 was received, the rest of the church program is in trouble.

Bonding programs, unfortunately, emphasize the "profit motive" instead of the "stewardship principle." Often purchased bonds are donated to the church, but some look upon bonds strictly as an investment and feel cheated if bonds are not redeemed in full. Yet the sale of bonds requires about as much effort and demand on loyalty as is needed to raise an outright gift of the same money.

Construction Funding

Own Resources

Churches should put forth every effort to have their own wisely invested cash on hand, received via offerings, property sales, memorials, and other sources, as a base for other funding. Interim financing can be eliminated by having as much cash on hand as possible.

Denominational Sources

Designated agencies, reposited usually within a denomination's home mission department, have the portfolio to grant loans to churches. Churches that invest some of their building fund monies in the agencies as "banks" are in a better position to secure loans. They have a line of credit.

Denominational agencies, on occasion, enter into financial alignments with banks or savings and loan companies to guarantee churches fulfillment of their payment commitments.

Another form of cooperation between a denominational agency and a bank was illustrated when the American Baptist Extension Corporation, Valley Forge, Pennsylvania, and the National Bank of Commerce of Seattle, Washington, combined efforts in 1962, lending the Mount Zion Baptist Church of Seattle $75,000 each at 6 percent, for a total of $150,000 to construct and equip a $300,000 educational unit.

Financial Institutions

Churches, as a rule, enhance their chances of securing loans for construction by depositing their funds in specified financial institutions, such as full service banks, savings and loan companies, and insurance companies.

Full service banks offer conventional loans. A few of these institutions have no moratoria on church construction loans. Savings and loan companies, on occasion, will schedule construction loans to churches if the church is in the city where the company's headquarters are located.

Caution in the administration of church loans must be exercised in two areas: reversionary clauses and special "pastoral clauses."

Black churches vehemently resist "reversionary clauses," or "claws," as one person put it, when the congregation borrows funds. White Baptist groups have "saved" some white churches from "fleeing" to other Baptist families by writing reversionary clauses in the loan contracts. This clause simply states that if the church ceases to exist, or wishes to become a part of another Baptist group, then the property would revert to the denomination granting the loan. Black Baptist churches feel this clause to be an "unBaptistic intrusion into the autonomy of the local church."

Furthermore, some financial institutions attempt to have the pastor sign a statement to the effect that he will not change pastorates during the life of the loan. Pastoral integrity demands that a pastor "occupy until He comes." However, no one wants to be fettered if the Lord directs one to another area of service. The man of God must be free to follow the leading of the Holy Spirit.

Philosophies of Financing Church Purchase, Renovation, or Construction

Men of another generation favored the concept of "paying as one went" for church improvement. This is understandable, for the most productive years of many of these clergy were spent during the depressed 1930s. "Pay as you go" is not feasible in this day and time, because of ever-escalating costs of labor and material.

The ideal concept for financing church construction might be labeled one-third (1/3), one-third (1/3), and one-third (1/3). The interpretation is one-third cash on hand, one-third to be raised by the congregation during the time of construction, and one-third to be secured during the life of the loan. Fortunate is the congregation that has one-third to one-half of the cost on hand for its building purposes.

While many white churches flee the inner cities and play "ring around the city," far too many black churches spend an inordinate amount of time, energy, and resources renovating and paying off the mortgages on dilapidated edifices. In light of this fact, a black congregation in Denver, Colorado, came up with a unique idea that all church buildings should be paid for only one time. This concept grew out of their concern that white congregations have bankrolled their "suburban captivity" through the sale of their ghetto properties. Arguing that the house of God, having been paid for one time, should not be bought or sold a second time, it was advocated that change of ownership would only entail the assumption of remaining mortgage payments and full responsibility for maintenance. One consultant even recommended that final title be conveyed only after a period of "payment" to the kingdom in the form of weekday programs of service to the community. As more and more black congregations ride the escalator to affluence, this concept may be just as revolting to them as it has been to the white church establishment.

Be that as it may, some vehicle of liberating congregations from their "unholy alliance to real estate" must be conceptualized and implemented.

Basic decisions are required of churches forced to change location for reasons of highway construction, urban renewal, institutional expansion, outgrowth of current facilities, and the irreparable condition of the present edifice.

To arrive at necessary decisions, questions should be raised by the congregation, such as:

—Is it cheaper to purchase an existing facility or erect another of equal size?

—Is more church space secured by purchase of an old building or by construction of the new?

—What other structures are available to congregations in search of a home?

    —storefronts?

    —warehouses?

    —theaters?

    —synagogues?

—In which direction/s are the members moving?

—What percent of current members would be lost by a church move?

—What anticipated percent of new people would be gained by a church move?

—Should the church remain in the same neighborhood, if not at the same site, or relocate in another part of town?

—Will a move make the church one with neighborhood or city-wide appeal?

—Can the church afford to move?

These and other queries should be thoroughly explored by a congregation faced with the problem of moving.

Architectural Services and Construction

Complexities of the construction industry mandate the hiring of an architect by a congregation planning massive renovation or construction of facilities. Therefore, a church should elect a building committee of seven to nine persons empowered to act on behalf of the congregation to facilitate the church building dream.

The Building Committee

The building committee should be small. A building council, comprised of several other committees as well, could be inaugurated by a church to serve as a representative sounding board for decision making.

What is the role of a building committee? First of all, it conducts hearings for the selection of an architect and reports the same to the congregation. Basic ingredients for the choice of architectural services should be: membership in the American Institute of Architects, experience in church design and construction, presence of a practicing architect within their congregation, and availability of black architects and willingness of non-black architects to hire black architects.

Secondly, the building committee develops a master building plan, based upon program needs, cost of construction, and the availability of funds. Other considerations confronting the committee are: what ministries are to be actualized in the facility, how much of the master plan and what portion of it should be erected first; and if the congregation changes location, should the sanctuary be constructed first to dramatize the presence of the church?

The building committee should demand that the new edifice announce to all that this is a Baptist church. In a black Baptist church, should the chancel be divided or the pulpit central? Where should the choir stand be located—behind the pulpit, divided in the chancel area, in the balcony, or to the side? Where should the baptistry be placed—behind the pulpit, in front of the pulpit, or in the entrance vestibule?

The following charts shed understanding on traditional and modified chancel arrangements in black Baptist churches.

CHART F

OLDER TRADITIONAL BLACK BAPTIST CHURCH CHANCEL ARRANGEMENT

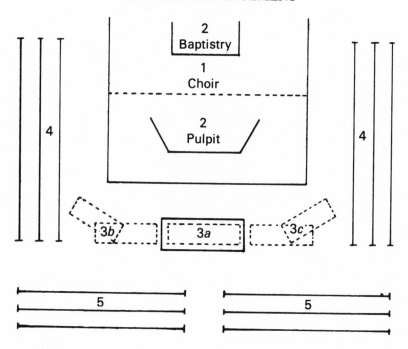

1. Place of choir stand—optional
2. Baptistry—central pulpit (centrality of the Word of God, not the preacher)
3. Three Tables of the church (please see Note with reference to Charts F and G.)
    a. Lord's Table (symbolic)—observance of Lord's Supper / Communion, presided over by the pastor; table for Communion reserved for sole purpose, and moved in on Communion Sundays; also the place of the offering table for the church or "Current Expense"
    b. Table of the Poor—support of the poor, presided over by the deacons
    c. Pastor's Table—support of the pastor, presided over by the deacons or trustees
4. "Amen Corners"—on either side of the chancel area
5. Seating

CHART G
(Variation of Chart F)
BLACK CHURCH USE OF A RECTANGULAR STYLE OF ARCHITECTURE

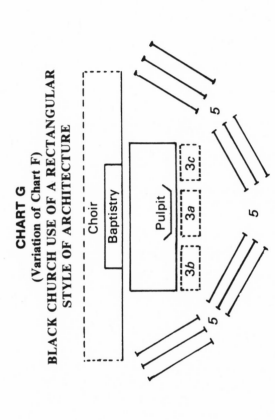

1. Baptistry
2. Pulpit

3. Three (Offering) Tables of the church
   a. Lord's Table—may occupy same place as Communion table
   b. Table of the Poor
   c. Pastor's Table

4. Choir area—optional
5. Seating for congregation

(NOTE: Tables 3b and 3c moved in for offerings; 3a as Communion table moved in on Communion Sundays.)

NOTE: With reference to Charts F and G.

The question is often raised at the ordination of preachers and deacons in traditional black Baptist churches, "What are the Three Tables of the church?" The candidates answer, "The Lord's Table, the Table for the Poor, and the Table for the Pastor." In today's church these tables, with the exception of the Lord's Table, are more symbolic than functional.

In another era, people brought their "gifts" and placed them on the respective tables. The emergence of the "envelope system" for church contribution encouraged congregants to place their donations for Current Expense, Benevolence, Education, Building Fund, Mortgage Retirement, and the like, in one envelope. As a result, only the Lord's Table remained central at the base of the pulpit. In churches where the members "walk around" for the offering on a regular or special basis, tables are often brought in to facilitate this act of worship.

To maintain the historicity of the symbolism of the Three Tables, one may discover the tables displayed in some form in fairly new sanctuaries or others under construction. The Three Tables depicted in Charts F and G may seem to be anchored to the floor architecturally. They are not. Basic to the observance of the rites and programs of the church is flexibility. Weddings, funerals, drama, and special music mandate judicious planning for the use of space at the base of the pulpit.

CHART H

Church sanctuaries with divided chancels and long naves were adopted by some black congregations who were either "aping" white modes of worship or constructing that which was "fashionable." Many black congregations have "inherited," from white congregations fleeing the city, the long-naved sanctuaries with a divided chancel. The style of architecture described is not "basic black."

Basic black church architecture is simple Early American "meeting house" building. This structure, rectangular in shape, lent itself to a seating arrangement where no one was far from the front and the movement of the "spirit" flourished. The "spirit" has a tendency to cool off, or disappear, in the long-naved, divided-chancel church.

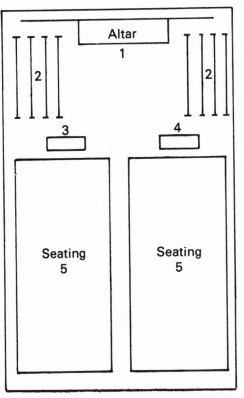

1. Altar
2. Divided choir stand
3. Pulpit
4. Lectern
5. Seating

Thirdly, the building committee works closely with the architect and informs the congregation of its stewardship by maintaining close alliance with the church financial officers, approving of architectural drawings, preliminary and final, understanding and acting on the plight of nonwhite contractors and construction workers, deciding on the types of bids to be secured, and receiving and approving progress reports from the architect.

What is the role of the architect? The architect translates into visual form the congregation's dream for a church within the members' self-concept of program and image and the limits of their financial capability; negotiates at all levels of the construction industry with contractors, both general and subcontractors, suppliers of material, organized labor to avert strikes and to include nonwhites in the work force, and supervises on-site construction and advises the building committee on progress and problems.

The architect, functioning as the church's building agent, usually charges approximately 8 percent of the total construction cost, broken down as follows:

2% for preliminary drawings

4% for final working drawings

2% for supervision during construction.

Problems of Black Contractors and Black Construction Workers

Black contractors and workers have in recent years become politicized and are demanding control of construction in ghetto areas, as well as their fair share of publicly financed projects wherever they exist.

Historically, blacks have been excluded from the construction industry work force, denied apprenticeship training, refused union membership, often forced to sit in union hiring halls while others went to work, and humiliated by rejection of reciprocal hiring agreements upon transferring from one area to another. As a result, black construction personnel refuse to be mistreated any longer by the industry and organize to protect themselves and secure their fair share of the available contracts and jobs.

Furthermore, black contractors have experienced difficulty in obtaining bonding, materials on credit, and loans from financial institutions. Inevitably blacks are forced to submit higher bids, thus rendering them incapable of competing on an equal footing with their white counterparts.

The plight of the black contractors is made worse by a lack of trust of them by the black community. Reasons for the lack of trust stem from bad experiences with black workers, a slave legacy causing many blacks to project black self-hatred on other blacks and accept the superiority of white workmanship. During the depression, a black woman switched from a black iceman to a white iceman. When asked about the change, she retorted, "The white man's ice is colder."

Recent improvements in the plight of black contractors are due to the availability of small business administration loans, the increased sensitivity to the problems due to confrontations, and the willingness of some white contractors to participate in "joint ventures" with black contractors. To avoid being "ripped off" by the large contractors, nonwhites have developed a "joint venture package" which includes the joint venture agreement, the actual bid-cost of construction, a completion/performance bond, and an affirmative action agreement on hiring.

Selection of a Contractor

By what methods are contractors selected? Methods for selecting a contractor have been standardized and guaranteed fair by a bid process, supervised by the architect. What are the types of bids commonly utilized?

Conventional Bid. By this process the contract to build would go to the lowest competent bidder. The conventional bid guarantees the best manner of ascertaining construction costs. However, for reasons enumerated earlier, nonwhite contractors are usually eliminated by this process.

Negotiated Bid. Under this arrangement, the church building committee selects a supervising general contractor, agrees to terms for supervisory services, and negotiates with the subcontractors at every level. Minority contractors stand fairer chances of inclusion under this practice and some financial savings can be effected.

Management Bid. The building committee, acting for the congregation, secures a contractor's license and hires a contractor. A fee ranging from 6 to 8 percent of construction cost is paid for managing the construction, saving on the contractor's profit and overhead. In essence, the arrangement involves a joint venture between church and contractor with the church as sponsoring agent and the contractor as managing agent effecting tremendous savings on construction cost. This joint venture requires a completion bond for every subcontractor. The building committee acts as managers doing basic paper work, controlling weak subcontractors by handling their materials, supplies, pay rolls, and fringe benefits paid to the union(s). This arrangement guarantees that the church will be in control at all times. Additional controls are inherent in the function of the architect, such as monitoring of work completion prior to progress payments to subcontractors.

The task of erecting a place of worship is of vital importance to a spiritual people. Controlling land to determine the destiny of that people is paramount. The control of the construction process as a resource for blacks is equally important, provided the church can obtain the talent and dedication to carry this responsibility properly. Therefore, the purpose for which a congregation erects a church should be accomplished with altruistic motives which go beyond the present. Generations yet unborn should benefit from our labors.

> Except the Lord build the house,
> they labour in vain that build it.
>
> (Psalm 127:1*a*)

8
Evaluation

Evaluation means assessing, making an appraisal of the situation, determining the worth of the program, and finding out just how well the "old ship of Zion" is navigating. In the usual situation, once the church determines its "success" in the past year, plans for the future are made. The whole theme of administration encompasses planning, budgeting, and evaluating.

The Need

The best administrator is one who plans the evaluation *before* beginning the administration. According to Thelma C. Adair:

> Evaluation really comes first, because if one takes the evaluation process seriously, it forces one to establish goals: to indicate procedures for the implementation of those goals, to identify the kind of persons and types of leadership skills needed plus the required budget, and then, to take a close look to see if what was attempted was achieved. Then the process of evaluation starts all over again.[1]

It is difficult to tell where one is to go if one does not know where one has been. It is difficult to judge the future if one does not take a look at the past, however pleasant or painful it may be to do so.

However, efficiency and evaluation are not an end in themselves. People must be viewed as of supreme worth. They are not cattle, as valuable as cattle may be today. People are at once those for whom Christ died and those for whom all institutions were created. Church programs were made for people and not people for programs.

All church procedures, practices, and programs are to be evaluated in the light of the following questions:

Can this black church practice be supported by Scripture?

Can this practice affirm or deny life?

Can it liberate or enslave?

Can it meet the needs of the whole person?

Can it dignify or demean?

Can this program include all of the people, or does it exclude some?
If a practice is inaugurated in place of an old, does it replace fully
what was taken away in the process of "rooting up and tearing
down"? (See Jeremiah 1:10.)

"All the things we do in the church are with people, by people, for
people and can't be done without people"[2]

Types of Evaluation

Informal Evaluation

Informal evaluation may take the form of gossip or feedback—
what the people have to say about the church worship service, the
general mood, and the fervor of the day's program.

At the conclusion of a Sunday worship experience, the minister
might be heard to say, "We had a great day; we fed everybody. The
spirit was here." Translated, it means that all segments of intelligence
benefited by the content, clarity, sincerity, and spiritual fervor.
Other questions to be considered are:

How was the crowd?

Was it the same, was it better, or did it fall off?

When the invitation to church membership was given following the
sermon, how many came forward to become new members?

Did the choir sing well?

Were the ushers in their places?

Did the nurses' corps find a remedy for the members who were
overcome?

Was the air conditioning too cold?

Was it uncomfortably hot in the sanctuary?

Was that special announcement made clearly?

Did the congregation leave orderly and prayerfully?

Was the worship service too long?

A church service need not last all day to be effective; but, on the
other hand, the brevity of the service may not necessarily add to the
quality. The black church lends itself to more singing, pulpit
instruction, altar prayer, and individual participation, which, of
necessity, run the worship experience past the one-hour "speed limit"
set by whites. The pastor must make judicious use of worship time—
not letting it drag on "ad infinitum" nor killing the spiritual fervor in
undue haste to conclude early. It is said that whites must
"understand" the sermon and worship service while blacks must
"feel" the sermon and worship experience. At its very best, the black

service requires more time, but evaluation can aid in avoiding useless length.

The urban situation, the telecasting of major sporting events, television prime-time spectaculars, plus radio and television ministries impact on all churches. Black congregations, especially those tending toward the middle class, have already felt the sting of competing factors on the lives of their people. Churches on the West Coast, for instance, are forced to compete at 10 A.M. with sport events televised from the East Coast at 1 P.M. For good or ill, evaluation demands that churches take stock of all forces impacting upon them and take a hard look at their basic historic commitments and act accordingly. This simply enables a church to give its basic commitments a high priority and keep its values in proper perspective.

Other informal evaluation may take the form of periodic praise and encouragement on the occasion of a birth, graduation, wedding, anniversary, special honor bestowed, or retirement. Praise begets praise. It never hurts to acknowledge the achievements of others and make them feel "ten feet tall."

Moreover, when group efforts have succeeded, it is well to take time to commend the congregation. Due to the pressures in daily employment, in some homes, and in the community, members need words of encouragement and comfort.

How discouraging it is to hear the words of an abusive, complaining, critical pastor from Sunday to Sunday! The people need the lift that only the fatherly pastor can give. While they must be reprimanded at times, let it be done sparingly.

Blessed are the people who encourage the pastor, especially when he is preaching in the black church. A sermon is dialogue to a great degree. There are "amens" and other expressions of approval, as the pastor preaches. After making some striking statement, the minister may say, "Am I right about it?" The answer from someone will be, "Yes, you are right about it." At other times the minister will say, "I know I am right about it," but it is far better to listen for spontaneous evaluation than to blow one's own horn.

The dialogue helps. It encourages, but it also evaluates. In some churches, "amens" may not abound, but the nodding of heads, attentive, smiling faces, and tears demonstrate as much support of the sermon as the vocal response. The pastor must be able to interpret response which is never monolithic. One elderly member of a large congregation in the Midwest would have one of the ushers hold her seat while she stood at the door where the pastor entered the pulpit each Lord's Day. "Let me hear from heaven this morning, Pastor!"

she would implore. Not one amen fell from her lips; not one tear fell from her eyes; not one sound was made by her feet. She sat almost motionless. At the end of the morning worship if she had heard from heaven, she would shake the pastor's hand and say, "Thank you." If it was a "low ceiling day" where the spirit was not too elevating, she would shake the pastor's hand and say, "I'm praying for you this week." That was evaluation.

There is also the *expectancy* type of informal evaluation. The sensitive and sensible pastor can be heard to say, "We reached a certain level of our objective, but next Sunday [or next year] we intend to achieve a higher goal." He makes clear what the people accomplished and where they are to go. Expectancy!

Formal Evaluation

When formal evaluation is used, there is data gathering. For example:

Who are the members? What are the age groups?

Where do they live?

Who are the active? Inactive? Why?

What are the economic needs of families?

Who attends church school, Youth Fellowship, Women's Missionary Society, Laymen's League, Usher Board, choir rehearsals?

What are the physical needs of the church?

What are the evangelistic and missionary needs?

What are the city land use plans for the church neighborhood?

What about zoning, property values?

Are freeways planned to displace the church building and families?

Data is gathered and reports are made to the pastor, official boards, or committees set up for the particular project. Dinners or special meetings are organized so that reports can be heard. They must not be filed away to gather dust.

The church annual meeting is the forum when all annual reports of importance are to be presented. The joint boards will have discussed and prepared reports and recommendations. Full reports of receipts and disbursements should be made on current expenses, building fund, and benevolence funds. This is not the time for a general oral statement or partial report. The full, printed or mimeographed report should be presented, with comparisons to previous years included for evaluation of trends.

Moreover, an auditor's report should be made or should be forthcoming.

While the matter of finance must always be straight and clear, it should be remembered that reports covering *all* auxiliaries and segments of the church program should be presented at the annual meeting. Money is not the only or even the primary concern.

Where possible, the annual reports should be printed or mimeographed and distributed to the membership.

Associations and Conventions request reports on the full church program. Forms on which data may be recorded are sent to the church office. The loyal and businesslike church administrator will fill out the reports in detail and return them to meet the deadline. Black churches often do not know their full strength because some churches do not keep records and send in reports.

Evaluation deals with the entire stewardship of the church—use of its time, talents, and financial resources. Stewardship is a word leadership must not be afraid to use. The member who will give God time and abilities will not object to giving money.

Formal evaluation must be done in terms of effectiveness. Where there are short- and long-term goals, the question must be faced, "Did we reach the first goals?" Then, "When and how do we proceed in the direction of the long-term goals?"

Environmental Evaluation

Environmental evaluation concerns itself with response and reaction to church programs and images from both inside and outside the church.

Response to Programs Within the Church

The manner in which members maintain church facilities presents one method of evaluation. When the members keep everything spic and span, it is because of the pastor's demands and/or the pride, ability, and integrity of the people. When men and women have special days for cleaning and repairs, there is deep loyalty to be admired or a measure of disinterest to be seriously considered.

The various anniversary programs and socials honoring the pastor for service beyond the call of duty provide another avenue of evaluation of response and effectiveness for the sensitive shepherd.

Support of Budget

Some people may not support the church budget simply because there is a general lack of interest. They have no antagonisms—they are just inactive members. But, by and large, in the black Baptist church, those who attend church regularly and do not support the budget indicate their dislike of the pastor or some policy. Some cease to support the church when not reelected to office and they lay the blame at the pastor's feet.

A solid support group can be recruited from among those who love the pastor. Those who give adequate support regardless of who the pastor is are few in number. Support of the church budget is an evaluation of the esteem for the leader.

Response to Programs Outside the Church

The treatment given the buildings and grounds by children in the block is one other evaluation of the pastor, the congregation, and its programs. Although both members and neighborhood children understand that the building is not the pastor's personal property, they refer to it as "Rev. Green's church."

How does the community view the church? What is the church's image in the community? Is the church a "silk stocking" church made up of so-called "big folks," meaning professionals and upwardly mobile people? Is the church a "Holy Ghost headquarters," known in the community as a place where the spirit is always high, even to the extent that a few people get happy over announcements? Is the church one that burns up or freezes up? Is the church a "church of what's happening now" with great appeal to youth or is it a place where more caskets are seen leaving the church than people entering it? Is it a "civil rights" church or a "Christian church"? Does the church care more for others than for itself? Is it a servant church? Are the people more concerned about their facilities and keeping them nice than dirtying their hands to help the community?

What impact would an announcement from the church's pulpit make on the community? What type of leadership does the community expect from the church? How does the community rate its churches? These and other concerns deal with environmental evaluation.

Effectiveness in Problem Areas

Acceptance/Rejection of Misfits/Problems

The average church member is conservative and slow to accept change. The words "change" and "something new" in the church give some members terrific headaches.

This may not be the case in other organizations, certainly not with regard to homes, flower gardens, automobiles, and clothes. But many Baptists feel that the church should be run like it was when they lived in the rural South. Little do they know that the rural southern church has changed and many of its programs are more progressive than some found in northern and West Coast urban churches.

Having stated that, it is only fair to state that a Baptist church can tolerate almost any type of "saint." Some dream dreams no mortal man has dreamed. Many pastors are "fools" for Christ's program. So long as "fools" do not "rip off" the people, members will receive a plan, try it, and suffer it with the "patience of Job."

A great host of lay persons may be commended for their long-suffering regarding some pastors, deacons, trustees, church school superintendents, missionary society presidents, choir directors, and other church leaders, who are square pegs in round holes (misfits). The measure of grace in any church is its tolerance for odd behavior among clergy and laity, as long as it is sincere.

Possibility of Church Outgrowing Leadership

In many instances small churches mushroomed in size during the Second World War. The migration of people from the South into the Far West, North, Northeast, and Midwest enabled many pastors to multiply their membership several times.

One veteran pastor said, "If you give a 'little' man a big job, he will not grow up to it, but he will cut it down to his size." These "small" pastors refuse to let the church increase either in large numbers or in program. On the other hand, pastors who continue their education in institutes, workshops, conferences, and extension courses are well able to keep abreast with the growing church.

Others are wise enough to choose trained and adequate staff, which enables the administration to keep abreast with every new innovation in black church life. One who can adjust to the new while maintaining the graceful past is well worth one's weight in gold. He who "cannot bend, go around, or run out of bounds sometimes" will find it very tough running through center on every play.

Pastors can and do remain at the helm of churches many years and stay as fresh as "tomorrow's milk" because they keep abreast of the times.

Administrative Evaluative Process

Consciousness Raising

The pastor and officers have the awesome task of creating a good climate for the raising of the fruit of commitment to the program. Much climate creation is done through positive preaching. The sermon is not meant to be used as a vehicle to fight people and to humiliate the opposition. That sacred time must be given to telling the story of Jesus and his love. "More flies can be caught with honey than vinegar." Every pastor needs to couple his dedication with love. Love outlasts anything. Love is contagious. Patient love and prayer change things. Good positive preaching, good fellowship, social programs, wholesome recreation, and a reputation for fairness and honesty will create the kind of climate needed.

Identifying Leadership

The evaluative process brings to the front many members who otherwise would never have been discovered. Some are shy; others are not sure what direction the pastor and officers wish to take. They are certain that they want no part of the "back to the early church" crusade. They have learned too much about the early church at Corinth and Crete, where problems could rival the worst of our day.

When extensive efforts are made to discover who the members are, what their skills are, and what their dedication may be, dependable leadership is found.

Providing Budget

When every area is appraised and assessed, it is not difficult to draw up a budget that will lift the program and win the support of the entire congregation. In other words, guarantee support-type evaluation by offering a clear and appealing budget.

The black church pastor has to be wise enough to guide his committee in keeping the budget within the reach or realization of his people. The financial campaign director must be watched closely lest he leave the church with goals and "commitments" which are above the reach of the people. Overambitious directors leave pastors suffering from unmet pledges.

Few high-pressure pastors enjoy long pastorates. Black people like progress, but the pastor must know how to progress gracefully without destroying the worshipful fellowship from Sunday to Sunday. Low-key church financing is best for a people who have been denied so many of the necessities of life and exploited by high-key entrepreneurs.

If the gospel is preached, if the program is above board, high pressure is unnecessary. The money will be raised. God has the power if we have the faith to move ahead. "Seek ye first the kingdom . . ." (Matthew 6:33).

Do not let bad budget strategy be confused with bad leadership and program, making it look as if the program is bad when only the funding approach was.

Nothing takes the place of involvement. Therein lies the genius of the black church with its five usher boards, twelve women's society circles, two basketball teams, a bowling league, four choirs, Willing Workers, Busy Bees, Ladies' Aid, Pulpit Club, Book Clubs, Nurses' Corps, Minute Men, Women's Chorus, and Men's Chorus.

Involvement is important. The pastor who is not afraid to let the people work will reap the dividends. If the young pastor has fears about leaders of groups becoming "dictators" and threatening his position, he need not worry. Their group will keep them humble, by their natural and perpetual evaluation.

Building on Past Experience

The administration must know how to profit from the past. The errors of yesterday can be averted today and indeed can provide wisdom for progress. The pastor must keep his mental record of the good and bad plays of the past so that the new game can be improved. One should not tackle in the same manner every time.

If separation of the boys from girls in church school, the youth fellowship meeting on Sunday afternoon, vacation church school, the rotation of deacons in office, or the appointment of leaders of all auxiliaries—if indeed any of these worked out poorly—the pastor, officers, and all involved must use the mistakes of the past to improve the future.

The pastor who is big enough to change or to admit error and mistakes is well on the way to maturity. When one studies oneself as well as one's people, and improves thereon, one is not far from the kingdom.

Moreover, that which has worked well need not be changed just for the sake of the new. Evaluation helps determine what needs to be kept as much as, if not more than, what needs to be changed.

9

Future Implications for Ministry

Administration, according to Archie Smith, Jr., may be defined as a socially organized and rationally planned process that seeks to implement and achieve agreed-upon objectives. Administration then is concerned with setting objectives and organizing the means to achieve such objectives. Administration is further concerned with the nature of choices that are open to individuals, the choices that are likely to contribute to effective performance.[1]

The black church, the *only* institution black people own under God, constantly confronted by problems greater than its resources to meet them, and comprised of a people who must be motivated spiritually to succeed in any venture, is called upon as never before to provide a base for the black community's actualization of its dream of self-determination.

What does the future hold for black Baptists, a classless society with a tradition of freedom and a free-flowing style of administration? What are the future implications of lay and pastoral relationships? What are future implications of power arrangements in black Baptist churches? What are future implications for church structure?

Implications for the Laity: Continuity or Change?

The black church is concerned with continuity—building beyond its days—by passing on its traditions to the next generation.

Socialization has been defined as a process whereby individuals learn requisite roles and internalize the attitudes, values, and behaviors appropriate to persons functioning as responsive, participatory members of their church community.[2]

From the perspective of the individual, socialization is the process whereby one develops an identity, learns to anticipate and evaluate, becomes self-aware (consciously experiences one's own behavior), and learns to relate to others. This process, continues Archie Smith,

Jr., is critical to the development of a community of solidarity—such as the black church. The individual must internalize the values of the church if the church is to become a living reality within one's very being.[3]

From the perspective of the black community, socialization is the process through which social and cultural perpetuation and continuity are achieved. The black church community cannot survive as a viable institution unless there is consensus among its majority regarding correct modes of behaving, thinking, interacting, and responding. If such consensus is to be achieved, individuals must internalize appropriate norms, values, attitudes, and behaviors.

The black church is concerned with nurturing values and norms in the individual, family, and peer groups, as well as affecting the total life of the community, as it brings its special vision to be pilgrim people.

Consequently, the black church is also concerned with keeping behavior within bounds. Hence, deviating behavior has to be held in check if the institution of the church is to be preserved. Thus, some administrative skills must be concerned with issues of social control, must seek to ensure a certain amount of conformity, and must discourage potentially disruptive behavior.

While institutional maintenance is important, and administrative skills necessary for such maintenance are basic, an eternal word from the Lord of the church proclaimed: "For whosoever will save his life shall lose it: but whosoever will lose his life for my sake, the same shall save it. For what is a man advantaged, if he gain the whole world, and lose himself, or be cast away?" (Luke 9:24-25).

New administrative methods of institutional maintenance must emerge in the near future. "The church must develop an economic system to sustain the spiritual," states Louis Smith.[4] It must develop an educational system to perpetuate the spiritual. In other words, the church must develop an economic base sustained by the faith of the fathers.

The question should be raised: How can institutional maintenance avoid the classical errors built into, or inherent in, the life cycle of institutions? Classical errors relate to how ad hoc "modus operandi" movements become institutionalized and formalized, and institutional maintenance becomes the top goal until supplanted by an internal reform movement.

Theology provides the church with the opportunity to avoid the inherent weaknesses of institutionalization. Theology constantly deals with the rejects of society, and the rejects/misfits often create the new society and replenish it. This is how theology keeps administration alive and makes the spiritual revolution continuous because it has not closed its doors on the people who need help and don't fit into things as they are.[5]

The strong have a built-in weakness; they preserve and perpetuate the status quo. Without the spiritual, education and economics must have constant revolution. Theology is continuous revolution, for the spiritual acts as a check and balance between education and economics. "Those who cannot deal with what is create the new."[6]

The meek shall inherit the earth (see Psalm 37:11; Matthew 5:5).

"The very stone which the builders rejected has become the head of the corner" (1 Peter 2:7, RSV).

The black church which conserves and preserves values which guarantee the continuity of the institution must also develop a process by which creative change is built into the very fabric of the institution. It is not a case of either/or, continuity or change, but both/and. The laity's task for the future is to enable the process of continuity/change.

Seminaries Without Walls

Churches must adopt and create a stronger lay ministry. Emphasis in lay ministry must concentrate on the areas of education, stewardship, missions, and evangelism based on a twenty-first-century world view. The pastor must lead the laity in their development by sharing leadership with them.

Black churches need to take a page from the book of the Jewish and Oriental people who, in an alien culture, developed educational vehicles to ensure community cohesiveness. "Seminaries without walls" could be such an instrument.

"Seminaries without walls," located in existing facilities, primarily churches, can be the focal point for the lay training. These seminaries would be functional, life-centered institutions which validate experience. The administrative evaluation process would be utilized to insure success of the venture. (See chapter 8.)

To develop the schools, target areas would be the senior citizens and those in the forty- to sixty-year age range, including the early retirees. Recruitment for the ministry should consider this target area as well.

The "seminary without walls" holds the seed of a very revolutionary concept that may enable churches to improve and redeem their neighborhoods and transform the institution of the church. The church must penetrate and permeate for good the urban vertical slums, the new apartments and condominiums, and the senior citizens' home. The church must lead in the rebuilding of the inner cities and commence by purchasing all available land. Innovative approaches to ministry in urban communities are a requisite for survival.

Tithing Path to Liberation

The principle of tithing (giving the Lord the first 10 percent of one's income) affords the black church an avenue to true liberation. To be free, one must strike the chains that bind one. Even though black people are an economically poor people, confronted by more problems than resources, tithing plus is a way out of the quagmire of despair, helplessness, and hopelessness.

Tithing plus provides the church with the opportunity to meet all institutional needs and to practice to its fullest extent in supporting missions at home and around the world.

In brief, tithing plus would enable the church to provide the following: housing for all its people; educational, technical, and professional training for all members; funding for those desiring to start in business or commence a profession; a full range of medical services for all its constituents from the cradle to the grave; employment of its people; succor, sustenance, and care for those of the community of faith and others incapable of caring for themselves or in trouble; and investment of its resources in enterprises committed to the enfranchisement rather than enslavement of its people.

Computers

We have moved into the "computer age." Our churches must consider the use of computers to keep all records up-to-date and easily accessible. Computer firms will provide instruction for church administrative officers. Have no hesitancy—full speed ahead for computers!

Implication for the Clergy

Continuing Education

What about the future? To function effectively on the cutting edge of affairs where change can occur demands that one's working tools be kept in excellent condition. Continuing education provides the opportunity to acquire freshness, maintain openness, and whet an appetite for the smorgasbord of new information in every field of inquiry.

The laity constantly engage in some form of educational pursuit just to keep up with the requirements of their employment. What if every black church demanded that its pastor take a specified number of continuing education courses each year and enroll in a six-weeks course of some type every three years? By this action, black churches would then be committed to the educational process and would lay to rest once and for all the anti-intellectual stereotype. Every black congregation should include an item in its budget for the pastor's continuing education or any other reasonable and intellectually sound venture. Time off for educational improvement should never be construed as vacation time.

At best, continuing education merely keeps its students abreast of current endeavors. But, the condition of the black community in just about every urban center warrants more preparation for social problem solving than is currently available. One must be a lifelong student, willing to learn *as much* as one can, *as long* as one can, *from whomever* one can, and *wherever* one can.

Bivocational Needs for Future Training of Clergy: Community Needs

Theological education should prepare seminarians to cope with the world of today and tomorrow. Somewhere in the core curriculum, new disciplines or new understandings informed by nontheological areas must be included. Moreover, black ministers, especially those either currently enrolled in a theological seminary or no more than five years out of the theological womb / tomb, should prepare themselves fully in another profession.

An increasingly complex society requires the clergy to have better tools with which to work. Black pastors must become bivocational, not for moonlighting considerations per se, but for meeting the challenge that will one day descend like an avalanche.

Biovocational ministries should include:

Education	Law
Urban Affairs	Medicine
Health Care Service	Psychology
Geriatrics	Business Administration
Child Care	Communications
Social Work	

By no means is the list exhausted, for almost any area of study can enrich the ministry.

Thomas Kilgore expressed the overpowering need for black churches of one thousand or more members to adopt a multiple ministry, for one pastor cannot cover all the ground and no one person has expertise in all areas.[7]

Educational Joint Ventures

Seminaries must place emphasis, Thomas Kilgore explained, on courses in practical theology—how to budget, sensing needs of staff, support of staff, and problems of dealing with staff in developing a team which can be developed through "field work." The black church with an increasing level of educational achievement must keep its wells of black spirituality open and renewed, and it must evolve into an efficient instrument capable of serving human needs. The church must have strong evangelistic preaching, excellent worship, and a sound business operation.[8]

Moreover, seminaries should explore the possibility of offering their degrees in conjunction with schools of social work, education, medicine, and law, so that graduates could conceivably receive together, for example, the Master of Divinity and the Master of Social Work degrees. Such combination of degrees will hasten the process of black liberation, self-actualization, and self-determination of ghetto communities.

Imagine a well-trained staff in a black Baptist church, responsible to the senior preaching pastor, consisting of an urban planner, an educational specialist, a minister of music, a psychiatrist, a counseling specialist, and children and youth ministers. Imagine such a full-time staff on the church's payroll with salaries comparable to secular society!

Seminarians with Master-Pastors

Seminarians will learn more and develop more quickly if given an opportunity to work with a "master-pastor." The day of fledgling clergy going to the woods and preaching their way back to town is a relic of yesteryear. Seminarians under the tutelage of master-pastors on occasion would learn more by osmosis than by absorption of some books. Not only would the young cleric add to the church staff while on assignment, but he also would develop friendships and relationships of lifetime duration.

Seminaries should search for these master-pastors and encourage their involvement in the life of their institutions.

Concept of Role

Increased educational opportunities, including travel, have broadened the outlook of many black clergy. As black clergypersons become more bilingual, bicultural, and bivocational, there will be increased pressures on them to be many more things to many more people in many more life situations. How then does the black preacher keep it all together? How does one avoid role confusion? How does one maintain one's identity as pastor?

The concept of "role," believes Archie Smith, Jr., consists of those behaviors typically performed by an individual in a particular situation. Roles are institutionalized. The congregation comes to "expect" certain things from its minister because the role is given a unique status.[9] (The history and expectations that accompany this role are described in chapters 1 and 2.) It seems that the crux of the issue is that the minister's role expands and undergoes change. A pastor must learn to function in a wide variety of complex roles that were traditionally not expected of him.

Both pastors and congregations have had to adjust to the expanding roles now open to the clergy. The Office of Economic Opportunity's war on poverty, the rash of "black courses" on both community college and university campuses, and the accessibility to consultancies of all types have provided some clergy with the challenge to express all their creative energies not utilized by churches with traditional outlooks, perspectives, and life-styles.

To the amazement of many clergy and congregations the pastors' effectiveness improved: church work was stimulated by the infusion of new information/data and methodologies, and the enrichment of pastor and people was evident for the entire community to behold. As a result, expectations were heightened.

On the other hand, far too many clergy are threatened by a well-informed laity and challenges too great for some to cope with. The threatened unfortunately often take refuge behind a dictatorial stance which renders any progress untenable and impossible. With greater congregational expectation pastors should relish the possibility of new beginnings. Any pastor who stimulates congregational growth, enjoys a modicum of success in enabling the membership to achieve its goals, effectively communicates the gospel, and treats all as equals need not be squeamish, feel threatened, or take refuge behind false fronts. Faithfulness has its own reward. A faithful pastor will be maintained as the leader of the congregation without question as long as he provides opportunity for growth, opportunity to share in decision-making processes, and opportunity to be a viable part of the tribe/clan/family/church.

The pressure, however, for the clergy to specialize in a complex role will increase; one may need to redefine the main thrust of one's ministry in certain areas, as may have already been done for example, in the areas of mental health, family and marriage counseling, and the like. The other option is for the senior pastor to be a "generalist," not a specialist, with a team (suggested earlier in this chapter). In the role of generalist, however, the pastor may experience role conflict from occupying two or more roles that have contradictory expectations.

Impact of Secularization

What will be the impact of secularization upon the black church and the black preacher? There is no question that as society changes and becomes more secularized, so too must the church come to terms with the changes taking place within and without. The church feels increased pressure to "keep up" with the times. But at what price? What about the black church? Surely, it is not immune from the process of secularization.

"Secularization," states Archie Smith, Jr., "generally means the process by which a religious orientation is gradually replaced by 'worldly' or scientific assumptions."[10] As the black community becomes more educated and more knowledgeable in worldly affairs, they too will experience continued challenges to answers which the traditional church has provided. The church can respond to the challenge by attempting to become more worldly-wise and sophisticated in the use of secular "techniques." But the task is perhaps far more awesome. The black Baptist church, and especially the worshiping community, will need more and more the creative leadership of a pastor-theologian, steeped in the faith of Afro-American Christian heritage, who is able to interpret the modern experience from a particular theological/administrative framework—one that has emerged from personal struggles as a contemporary person of faith. Although the pastor may become a specialist or a generalist, one must never cease to be a pastor/theologian/administrator. The pastor/theologian/administrator must proclaim:

There is a balm in Gilead (see Jeremiah 8:22).

There is a word from the Lord (see Jeremiah 37:17).

The past is behind one. The present is upon one and the future is yet to be. The future is incomplete, for in the words of George B. Thomas, "We are incomplete."[11]

The emerging Black church, successor to the Negro and Mulatto versions, possessing an informed and strong laity, with resources resulting from sound stewardship, with pastors steeped in the history, culture, and faith of their people, who are true to its historic prophetic witness, equipped with sound and tested administrative principles, can emancipate not only black people but all people. This church will lead mankind to the Eternal's holy hill. Assembled before the Lord of history, his glory shall be revealed, and all flesh shall see and experience their salvation/liberation together.

Suggested Readings

Church Administration

Adams, Arthur M., *Effective Leadership for Today's Church.* Philadelphia: The Westminster/John Knox Press, 1978.

Agar, Frederick A., *The Deacon at Work.* Valley Forge: Judson Press, 1980.

Asquith, Glenn H., *Church Officers at Work.* Valley Forge: Judson Press, 1951.

Burt, Steve, *Activating Leadership in the Small Church.* Valley Forge: Judson Press, 1988.

Drucker, Peter F., *Management: Tasks, Practices, Responsibilities.* New York: Harper & Row, Publishers, 1973, 1974.
FOR PAGE 139:

Grenell, Zelotes, and Goss, Agnes Grenell, *The Work of the Clerk.* Valley Forge: Judson Press, 1987.

Griggs, Donald L., and Walther, Judy McKay, *Christian Education in the Small Church.* Valley Forge: Judson Press, 1988.

Harrison, Paul M., *Authority and Power in the Free Church Tradition: A Social Case Study of the American Baptist Convention.* Carbondale, Ill.: Southern Illinois University Press, 1971.

Hiscox, Edward T., *The Hiscox Guide for Baptist Churches.* Valley Forge: Judson Press, 1964.

Johnson, Alvin D., *The Work of the Usher.* Valley Forge: Judson Press, 1986.

Lindgren, Alvin J., *Foundations for Purposeful Church Administration.* Nashville: Abingdon Press, 1965.

Mapson, J. Wendell, Jr., *The Ministry of Music in the Black Church.* Valley Forge: Judson Press, 1987.

Maring, Norman H., and Hudson, Winthrop S., *A Baptist Manual of Polity and Practice, Revised Edition.* Valley Forge: Judson Press, 1963, 1991.

McLeod, Thomas E., *The Work of the Church Treasurer.* Valley Forge: Judson Press, 1987.

McNeil, Jesse Jai, *Minister's Service Book.* Grand Rapids: William B. Eerdmans Publishing Co., 1982.

Merrill, Richard Dale, *The Church Business Meeting.* Valley Forge: Judson Press, 1981.

Naylor, Robert E., *The Baptist Deacon.* Nashville: Broadman Press, 1955.

Nichols, Harold, *The Work of the Deacon and Deaconess.* Valley Forge: Judson Press, 1964.

Robert, Henry M., *Robert's Rules of Order Revised.* New York: Morrow, William and Co., Inc., Publications, Inc., 1971.

Sawyer, David R., *Work of the Church: Getting the Job Done in Boards and Committees,* Valley Forge: Judson Press, 1986.

Smith, Wallace Charles, *The Church in the Life of the Black Family.* Valley Forge: Judson Press, 1985.

Tibbetts, Orlando L., *The Work of the Church Trustee.* Valley Forge: Judson Press, 1987.

_____ , *How to Keep Useful Church Records.* Valley Forge: Judson Press, 1983.

Black Church Studies

Bennett, Lerone, Jr., *What Manner of Man: A Biography of Martin Luther King, Jr., 1929-1968*. Chicago: Johnson Publishing Company, Inc. 1968.

Cleage, Albert B., Jr., *Black Christian Nationalism: New Directions for the Black Church*. Detroit: Luxor Publishers of the Pan-African Orthodox Christian Church, 1987.

Cone, James H., *Black Theology and Black Power*. New York: The Seabury Press, Inc., 1969.

Drake, St. Clair, *The Redemption of Africa and Black Religion*. Chicago: Third World Press, Atlanta Institute of the Black World, 1970.

Jones, Edward L., *Profiles in African Heritage*. Seattle: Edward-Lynn Jones & Associates, 1972.

King, Martin Luther, Jr., *Where Do We Go from Here: Chaos or Community?* New York: Harper & Row, Publishers, Inc., 1967.

_____ , *Why We Can't Wait*. New York: New American Library, 1987.

Lincoln, C. Eric, *Race, Religion, and the Continuing American Dilemma. The Black Experience in Religion*. New York: Farrar, Straus, & Giroux, Inc., 1984.

Mays, Benjamin Elijah, and Nicholson, Joseph W., *The Negro's Church*. Salem, N.H.: Ayer Co. Publishers, Inc., 1969.

Mbiti, John S., *African Religions and Philosophy*. Portsmouth, N.H.: Heinemann Educational Books, Inc., 1969.

Mitchell, Henry H., *Black Preaching*. New York: Harper & Row, Publishers, Inc., 1979.

Stallings, James O., *Telling the Story: Evangelism in Black Churches*. Valley Forge: Judson Press, 1988.

Thurman, Howard, *Jesus and the Disinherited*. Richmond, Ind.: Friends United Press, 1981.

Washington, Joseph R., Jr., *Black Sects and Cults*. Landham, Md.: University Press of America, 1984.

_____ , *Black Religion: The Negro and Christianity in the United States*. Landham, Md.: University Press of America, 1984.

Washington, Preston Robert, *God's Transforming Spirit: Black Church Renewal*. Valley Forge: Judson Press, 1988.

Wilmore, Gayraud S., *Black Religion and Black Radicalism: An Interpretation of the Religious History of Afro-American People*. Maryknoll, N.Y.: Orbis Books, 1983.

Yette, Samuel F., *The Choice: The Issue of Black Survival in America*. Silver Spring, Md.: Cottage Books, 1982.

Appendix

A Sample Church Constitution

ARTICLE I

NAME

The name of this Church shall be the . . .

ARTICLE II

PURPOSE

The purpose of this congregation is to give visible form to that faith and fellowship to which God has called his people. We acknowledge ourselves to be a local manifestation of the universal church through which Jesus Christ continues to minister to the world by his Holy Spirit. We shall seek to fulfill this calling through corporate worship services, through a program of Christian nurture by which our members may be built up in their faith and love, through proclamation of the Gospel by word and deed, and through ministering to human need in the name of Christ.

ARTICLE III

POLICY

Section I:
The government of this Church is vested in the members who compose it, and, as such, it is subject to the control of no other

ecclesiastical organization. Also, none of its Boards or Committees can usurp its executive governmental or policy-making powers.

Section II:
It shall maintain affiliation and cooperation with the _____ Association, the American Baptist Churches in the U.S.A.; the National Baptist Convention, U.S.A., Inc., and its affiliates.

Section III:
This Church shall also cooperate with the National Council of Churches of Christ, and the World Council of Churches of Christ.

ARTICLE IV

DOCTRINE

This Church accepts the Scriptures of the Old and New Testaments as the inspired record of God's revelatory actions in human history and as the authoritative basis for its doctrine and practice.

This Church also has adopted the following covenant as a means by which its members may express their intent to accept the lordship of Jesus Christ in the affairs of daily life. This document shall be subject to revision by the congregation as new insights from the Word of God shall indicate ways in which our faith and life may be brought into closer accord with the teachings of the Scriptures.

CHURCH COVENANT

MINISTER: It being made manifest by God's Word that God is pleased to walk in a way of covenant with his people, he promising to be their God and they promising to be his people:

PEOPLE: We, therefore, desiring to worship and serve Him, and believing it to be our duty to walk together as one body in Christ, do freely and solemnly covenant with God and with one another, and do bind ourselves in the presence of God, to acknowledge God to be our God and us to be his people; to cleave unto the Lord Jesus, the great Head of the Church, as our only King and Lawgiver; and to walk together in brotherly love, the Spirit of God assisting us, in all God's ways and ordinances as they have been made known or shall be made known unto us from his holy

Word; praying that the God of peace, who brought from the dead our Lord Jesus, may prepare and strengthen us for every good work, working in us that which is well pleasing in his sight, through Jesus Christ our Lord, to whom be glory forever and ever. Amen.

ARTICLE V

CHURCH MEMBERSHIP

Section 1—Admission of Members

Persons may be received into membership by any of the following methods, subject in each case to the recommendation of the Membership Committee and the vote of the Church.

By Baptism:

A person who confesses Jesus Christ as Lord and Savior and adopts substantially the views of faith and principles of this Church and is baptized by immersion may be received into the fellowship of the Church.

By Letter:

A person who is in substantial accord with the views of faith and the principles of this Church may be received by letter from any other Christian church.

By Experience:

A believer of worthy character who has formerly been a member of a Christian church, but who for a sufficient reason cannot present a letter from that church, but who is in substantial accord with the views of faith and principles of this Church may be received upon statement of experience.

By Restoration:

A person who has lost membership may be restored to membership upon recommendation of the Church Membership Committee and the vote of the church.

By Watchcare:

A person who is a member of another Christian church but sojourning in this community for a brief period of time may be received into the membership of the Church for a three- to six-month period. Students may unite under watchcare while they are enrolled in a local institution of learning.

All applications for admission to Church membership shall be presented in the form of a recommendation from the Church Membership Committee.

Section 2—Termination of Members
By Letter:

Any member in good standing who desires a letter of dismission and recommendation to any other Baptist church may receive it upon his request and upon the recommendation of the Board of Deacons and the vote of the Church. The church to which membership is requested shall be named in the request and the letter shall be sent to the pastor or clerk of that church. Such letter shall be valid only for six (6) months after its date, unless reviewed, and this restriction shall be stated in the letter.

By Statement:

Any member in good standing may be granted a certificate of standing for the purpose of associating himself with any evangelical church other than a Baptist church.

By Exclusion:

Should any member become an offense to the Church and to its good name by reason of immoral or unchristian conduct, or by consistent breach of his covenant vows, the Church may terminate his membership, but only after due notice and hearing before the Board of Deacons, and after faithful efforts have been made to bring such a member to repentance and amendment.

By Suspension:

The Board of Deacons should prepare from year to year a list of those members who have for a period of two (2) or more years failed to participate in the service of worship, financial support, or the educational program of the Church without valid excuse. If they are satisfied that the persons so described cannot be reclaimed, they shall present to the Church a recommendation that these delinquent members be erased from the membership roll. Upon such action being taken by the Church, said members shall thereafter cease to be members of this Church.

By Death.

ARTICLE VI

PASTOR

Section 1:
The pastor shall preach the gospel, administer the ordinances, watch over the membership, and have charge of the spiritual welfare of the congregation and the stated services of public worship. The pastor shall be an ex-officio member of all Boards and Committees of the Church and its auxiliary organizations.

The pastor shall be the Moderator and shall preside at all business meetings of the Church except when good taste dictates otherwise.

Section 2:
When it is necessary to call a pastor, the Church shall select a representative Pulpit Committee of seven (7) members. It shall be the duty of this Committee to take necessary steps to secure a pastor. The Committee shall investigate the merits of every candidate under consideration in regard to personal character, education, ministerial record, and preaching ability in determining his fitness for said pastorate. When a suitable candidate is found, the Committee shall recommend that person to the Church for consideration.

Section 3:
The call of a pastor shall come before the Church at a regularly called business meeting, notice of such meeting and its purpose having been read from the pulpit on two (2) successive Sundays. A vote of two-thirds (2/3) of the members present and qualified to vote shall be necessary to extend a call. Only one candidate shall be presented to the Church at any one regular meeting. The vote shall be by written ballot.

Section 4:
The pastor shall be called for an indefinite period of time. The salary shall be fixed at the time of the call and may be changed by vote of the Church at any regular business meeting, provided that such a change has been considered by the Board of Deacons and Trustees in a joint meeting. The salary shall be paid in weekly installments. The pastor shall be given an annual vacation of not less than four (4) weeks with pay.

Section 5:

A pastor's term of office may be ended upon ninety (90) days of notification on the part of the pastor or of the Church by mutual consent. Termination of the office shall be voted on at a regularly called business meeting, notice of such meeting and its purpose having been read from the pulpit on two (2) successive Sundays. A vote of a majority of the members present and qualified to vote, providing there be present a quorum of fifty (50) members, shall make a valid termination of said office.

Section 6:

In the event the Church considers it wise to have one or more assistant pastors, the pastor is given authority to select such an assistant, subject to consent and approval of the Church body.

ARTICLE VII

CHURCH OFFICERS

The elected officers of this Church shall be:
Section 1: Pastor and Assistant(s), if any, whose duties are set forth in Article VI, Section 1.

Section 2: Clerk

A clerk shall be elected at each annual meeting to serve for one year. The clerk shall keep a complete record of the transaction of all business meetings of the Church. This shall be read for approval at the next following business meeting. The clerk shall keep a record of the names and addresses of the members, with dates and manner of admission and termination, also a record of baptisms, and a list of those suspended. The clerk shall notify all officers, committee members, and delegates of their election and appointment. The clerk shall issue letters of termination and recommendation voted by the Church, preserve on file all communications and written reports, and give legal notice of all meetings where such is required by this Constitution. The clerk shall assist in preparing denominational reports. The clerk shall deliver immediately to his or her successor all books and records for which he or she has been responsible as clerk.

Section 3: Assistant Clerks

There shall be two (2) assistant clerks elected annually to serve in the

absence of the clerk, receive new members into the Church, and serve
on the Membership Committee.

Section 4: Treasurer

The treasurer shall be elected at each annual meeting to serve one (1)
year. The treasurer shall have custody of the funds of the Church and
all the deposits made in the name of the Church, and all checks drawn
by the treasurer shall be in the name of the Church.

1. The treasurer shall receive all monies belonging to the Church,
   except the Fellowship Fund or others so designated by the
   Church.
2. The treasurer shall keep separate accounts of all funds raised or
   contributed for particular purposes. NO funds shall be disbursed
   by the treasurer except for the purpose for which they were raised
   or contributed.
3. The treasurer shall have custody of the securities, investments,
   title papers, and other valuable documents of the Church.
4. The treasurer, within twenty-four hours, shall deposit the monies
   received, in a bank selected by the Trustee Board.
5. Funds received for the support of the Church and for the
   reduction of the Church indebtedness shall be disbursed by the
   treasurer only on the order of the Board of Trustees. This shall be
   expedited only upon warrants attested by the signature of the
   chairman of the Board of Trustees and the Financial Secretary.
6. The treasurer shall submit to the Trustees, upon their request,
   information as to the condition of the treasury.
7. The treasurer shall keep a summary of the financial standing of the
   Church before the members, through bulletins or other publications, by posting on the bulletin board, or by a quarterly letter.
8. The treasurer shall submit to the Church an itemized report of
   receipts and disbursements, showing the actual financial condition of the Church at each quarterly meeting. At the annual
   meeting of the Church, upon receipt of the treasurer's report, the
   books shall be submitted to the auditors.
9. The treasurer of this Church shall be bonded.

Section 5: Financial Secretary

The financial secretary shall be elected at each annual meeting to
serve for one (1) year. It shall be the financial secretary's duty:

1. To furnish each member of the Church envelopes for contribution
   to Church funds; to keep a record of pledges made; to collect all

monies contributed; to keep a correct account thereof between the Church and its members.

2. To keep an accurate account of all monies received by the Church and to send a weekly statement to the treasurer.
3. To send out personal statements to all members once a year, listing their gifts.
4. To report to the Trustees an account of the matters pertaining to his/her office at each Trustee meeting or upon request of the Trustees.
5. To report to the Board of Deacons the names of those members who have failed to make any contributions of record toward Church expenses or funds.
6. To submit his/her records upon receipt of the Church to the auditors at the annual meeting.
7. To keep an accurate record of the receipts and disbursements of all auxiliaries, groups, and boards, except the Fellowship Fund.
8. The financial secretary shall be bonded.

The secretary of the Church may also serve as the financial secretary. The financial secretary shall also be an ex-officio member of the Finance Board.

ARTICLE VIII

ADVISORY COUNCIL

There shall be an Advisory Council consisting of the elected officers of the Church, all members of the Diaconate, Trustees, and Finance Boards, Board of Education, Board of Missions and Evangelism, chairmen of all committees, and presidents of all auxiliary organizations. Three members-at-large shall be elected from the Church body annually.

All matters of importance shall be considered by the Advisory Council before being presented to the Church. The Council shall appoint, subject to ratification by the Church, all standing committees. It shall seek to coordinate the activities of the Church, including long-range planning.

The Council shall undertake to strengthen the total work of the Church, its Boards, Committees, and Auxiliary Organizations. It shall meet quarterly or as often as necessary.

The quarterly meeting of the Advisory Council shall take the place of the quarterly church meeting. However, special church meetings may be called to meet needs as they arise.

ARTICLE IX

BOARDS

Section 1: Deacons
There shall be a board of seven (7) or more Deacons. The Deacons shall be ordained to their work according to Acts 6:1-8 and 1 Timothy 3:8-13.

As the need arises, this office may be filled upon recommendation from the Pastor and Deacon Board to the Church. This recommendation is to be read on two (2) consecutive Sundays prior to any quarterly business meeting of the Advisory Council. At such a business meeting, recommendations may be submitted by the body.

Those persons to be accepted by the Church to fill the office of a Deacon must pass the test of moral qualifications as listed in the above-mentioned Scriptures.

Any member who feels that a candidate is not suited for the office must apprise the Church and confront the candidate with a charge at a special meeting to determine qualifications. One who so confronts must observe two (2) requirements:
1. Specific charges must be brought and stated in writing, presenting evidence that is clear, cogent, and convincing, as to its truth.
2. Remember the words of Jesus, "He that is without sin, let him cast the first stone."

Persons passing the test will be placed on probation for six (6) months, in which time they will undergo rigorous training and preparation for the task. At the end of this period and upon recommendation to the Church, the candidate or candidates shall be ordained.

Deacons shall hold office as long as they shall faithfully discharge their duties.

Any Deacon who, for a period of three (3) months, fails to perform the duties of his office faithfully automatically vacates the same. The Church may, for good and sufficient cause, remove any Deacon from office.

The Board shall choose annually a chairman, a vice-chairman, a secretary, and a treasurer and shall meet regularly each month.

Special meetings may be called by the chairman or the secretary, who shall notify other board members. A majority of the members shall constitute a quorum.

The Board shall in every way assist the pastor; cooperate with the pastor in providing the pulpit supply and the leaders of the prayer meeting; visit the members; care for the sick, needy, and distressed members of the Church; use the Fellowship Fund as may be needed.

The Board shall promote Christian instruction and ministry to the Church membership; provide for the Ordinances and aid in their administration; make a written report at each quarterly meeting of the Advisory Council on the Fellowship Fund and the matters in its charge.

Section 2: Deaconesses
The Board of Deaconesses shall assist the Pastor in developing the spiritual life of the women and girls of the Church for the best possible Christian service. It shall cooperate with the Pastor and the Board of Deacons in visiting the members; in the care of the sick, needy, and distressed members of the Church; in the disbursement of the Fellowship Fund; and in the preparation of the observances of the Ordinances of the Church.

Deaconesses shall hold office as long as they shall faithfully discharge their duties.

Any Deaconess who, for a period of three (3) months, fails to perform faithfully the duties of her office automatically vacates the same. The Church may, for good and sufficient cause, remove any Deaconess from office.

The Board shall choose annually a chairman, a vice-chairman, a secretary, and a treasurer and shall meet regularly each month.

Special meetings may be called by the chairman or the secretary, who shall notify other members. A majority of the members shall constitute a quorum.

Section 3: Trustees

There shall be a Board of eleven (11) Trustees, one of whom shall be the Church Financial Secretary, and one of whom shall be the Church Treasurer.

One-third (1/3) of the trustees, except the financial secretary and the treasurer, shall be elected at each annual meeting for a term of three (3) years. Consecutive terms shall be limited to two (2).

The Board shall choose annually a chairman, a vice-chairman, and a secretary and shall meet regularly each month. Special meetings may be called by the chairman or by the secretary who shall notify the other members. A majority of the members shall constitute a quorum.

The Board shall hold in trust all property belonging to the Church and shall take all necessary measures for its protection, management, and upkeep. It shall determine the use of the Church buildings for all extra or secular purposes, but it shall have no power to buy, mortgage, lease, or transfer any property without specific vote of the Church authorizing such action. It shall designate the bank where the funds of the Church shall be deposited. All bills authorized by the Church shall be cleared through the Board of Trustees before payment is made. It shall, when so instructed by the Church, secure the services of a custodian at such salary as is authorized by the Church and secure from him acceptable service. It shall also, when instructed by the Church, secure the services of a church secretary. It shall perform such other duties as are imposed upon it by the Church and State.

The Board shall supervise ways and means of raising the necessary funds for the support of the Church and for benevolences. It shall supervise the disbursements of these funds as appropriated. It shall make written reports to the Church at the quarterly business meeting and at such other times as may be desired.

Section 4: Finance

There shall be a Finance Board of six (6) members, one-third (1/3) of whom shall be elected at each annual meeting for a term of three (3) years. Consecutive terms shall be limited to two (2).

It shall act as a budget committee for the Church and shall devise means and solicit subscriptions for the revenue of the Church. It shall report all pledges to the Financial Secretary. The Chairman of the Trustee Board and the Church Financial Secretary shall serve as ex-officio members of this Board. This Board shall lead and direct the financial efforts of the Church.

This Board shall elect a chairman and secretary and shall meet quarterly and whenever the need arises.

Section 5: Christian Education
The Board of Christian Education shall consist of twelve (12) elected members, one-third (1/3) of whom shall be elected each year for a term of three (3) years. Consecutive terms shall be limited to two (2).

In addition to the elected members, the following persons shall serve by virtue of their office as ex-officio members with voting privileges. They are: the Pastor, the Director/Minister of Christian Education, and the general Superintendent of the Church School.

The work of the Board will be divided into the following areas: Children, Youth, Young Adult, Adult, Leadership Development, Education for Missions, Athletics and Recreation, the Church Arts, Library, and Audio/Visual. A member of the Board shall be responsible for each of these areas. The chairman of each area will function with and through committees, particularly the age-group chairmen. In addition to this, the Board will operate with task groups. A task group is any ad hoc committee with limited tenure. This is a task force appointed to accomplish a particular job within a given length of time.

The Board shall be responsible for the ORGANIZATION, ADMINISTRATION, AND SUPERVISION of the entire education program of the Church.

It shall be responsible for:

DEVELOPING and INTERPRETING to the constituency of the Church the EDUCATIONAL OBJECTIVES or GOALS;

STUDYING the educational needs of the Church and for making decisions concerning time schedules, educational use of housing and equipment, and the elimination or addition of classes or organizations;

DISCOVERING, ENLISTING, TRAINING, and APPOINT-ING all Church educational workers;

COORDINATING and APPROVING the outreach program of the groups and organizations under its jurisdiction;

EVALUATING, DETERMINING, and SUPERVISING the curriculum of the educational program;

PREPARING the educational budget of the Church and submitting the same to the Finance Board.

The Board shall be organized promptly, following the annual election. It shall elect from its own membership a chairman, an assistant chairman, and a secretary. The Board shall meet monthly at a stated time. Special meetings may be called by the chairman, or the Director of Religious Education, if any. The Board will prepare a report of the activities of the program to be submitted at the quarterly meeting of the Advisory Council and the annual meeting.

The Board of Christian Education shall appoint the counselors for youth and shall interview and approve the teachers for the Church School. The Board shall nominate the leaders for the Church School and Baptist Fellowship groups.

Section 6: Board of Missions and Evangelism
The Board of Missions and Evangelism shall consist of nine (9) elected members, one-third (1/3) of whom shall be elected each year for a term of three (3) years. Consecutive terms shall be limited to two (2). The chairmen of the boards of Deacons, Deaconesses, Trustees, Christian Education, Finance, and the presidents of the Brotherhood and Woman's Society shall be non-voting members. An Assistant/Associate in the Ministry, if any, may be assigned to work with this Board as an ex-officio member.

This Board shall promote interest in missions at home and internationally. It shall accept and reach a high goal of missionary giving and shall cooperate with regional and national groups on missionary cooperation to promote giving.

This Board shall cooperate with the Pastor in providing practical ways for implementing the evangelistic mission of the Church, such as neighborhood visitation, preaching services, and study groups, etc.

This Board shall plan and administer the Missions and Evangelism Budget. This Board shall be organized promptly following the annual election. It shall elect from its own membership a chairman, a vice-chairman, and a secretary. The Board shall meet monthly at a stated time. Special meetings may be called by the chairman.

The Board will prepare a report of activities to be submitted at the quarterly Advisory Council meeting and the annual Church Meeting.

Section 7: Office Tenure
After a Church member has held office for two (2) consecutive terms, he or she shall not be eligible for reelection to the same office for a period of one (1) year after the expiration of the second term, except Deacons and Deaconesses.

Any officer who for a period of three (3) months shall fail to perform faithfully the duties pertaining to the office thereby automatically vacates said office. The Church has the power, for good and sufficient cause, to remove from office any officer.

Resignations from elected officers shall be made in writing to the Church by giving notice to the Advisory Council.

ARTICLE X

COMMITTEES

Section 1: Church Paper
The Church Paper Committee will see that the Church newspaper is edited, produced, and distributed.

Section 2: Communications and Publicity
The Communications and Publicity Committee, appointed by the Advisory Council and representative of the total Church body, shall make known what the Church stands for and what it has to offer, by use of newspapers, radio, television, and other available media.

Section 3: Committee on Christian Social Concern

The Committee on Christian Social Concern, appointed by the Advisory Council, shall provide information, encouragement, and channels by which the lordship of Christ may be acknowledged, as it relates to social issues in the family, community, nation, and world.

Section 4: Social Committee

The Social Committee, appointed by the Advisory Council, shall promote fellowship within the Church and, when so requested by the Pastor, shall be responsible for entertainment. It shall help members become better acquainted.

Section 5: Music Committee

The Music Committee is charged with the responsibility of providing for and maintaining a musical program of excellence for the Church. The Music Committee, appointed by the Advisory Council, shall cooperate with the Pastor and Assistant Minister of Music in the selection of an organist, instrumentalists, and choir directors, and in the securing of musicians for the various Church services.

The Music Committee shall be comprised of seven (7) members, plus the Pastor, Assistant Minister of Music, and directors of the choirs.

The Music Committee shall plan and review the Church musical program for the year; maintain a file of all the musicians in the Church; provide training experiences for church musicians, including workshops, seminars, etc.; select hymnals to be used by the Church for worship; provide for the robing of the choirs; and prepare the music budget of the Church and submit the same to the Finance Board.

Section 6: Membership Committee

The Membership Committee, appointed by the Advisory Council, shall meet with the proposed new members to orient them. It shall recommend to the Church those who are deemed ready for membership. It shall keep an accurate record and account of the membership of the Church.

Section 7: Ushering

Ushering shall be under the supervision of the Advisory Council. The ushers shall attend to the seating of the congregation and to the receiving of the offering.

Section 8: Nominating Committee

The Nominating Committee shall be appointed by the Advisory Council at the third quarterly meeting of the Advisory Council. It shall be a representative committee and shall prepare a list of those qualified to fill various offices. It shall interview each nominee proposed and ascertain his or her willingness to serve if elected. The committee shall nominate one or more persons for each office to be filled and report the names to the church at least two (2) weeks before the election is to be held.

All auxiliaries shall submit the slate of their officers to the Nominating Committee to be placed on the ballot for ratification by the church.

Section 9: Auditing Committee

The Auditing Committee, appointed by the Advisory Council, shall audit or have audited the financial records of the Church at least once each year and shall make a report in writing to the Advisory Council at the first quarterly meeting.

Section 10: Pulpit Committee (see Article VI, Section 2)

Section 11: Special and General Committees

Special and General Committees shall be appointed by the Advisory Council as need shall arise. The principle of rotation in effect for Boards shall apply to committees and committee chairmen.

Any committee member who for a period of three (3) months shall fail to perform faithfully the duties pertaining to the office thereby automatically vacates the same. The Church has the power, for good and sufficient cause, to remove from office any committee member.

Resignations of committee members shall be made in writing by giving notice to the Advisory Council.

ARTICLE XI

ELECTIONS

Section 1: Time

The annual election of officers shall be held during the annual meeting of the Church, which shall be on the second Friday evening in January.

Section 2: Qualifications of Voters

All matters pertaining to the purchase, sale, or mortgaging of property shall be voted on only by members in good standing, who are of legal age. On all other matters, members in good standing, who are fifteen (15) years of age or older, are entitled to vote.

Section 3: Procedure

At least two (2) weeks before the election, the Nominating Committee shall present to the Church the names of one or more persons for each office to be filled. This ballot is to be posted so that all members might know those who are being placed in nomination. It shall be the privilege of any two (2) members, qualified to vote, to place in nomination the name of any eligible person for any office, not so nominated, and such nomination shall be placed on the ballot. No nominations shall be made from the floor at the time of election, but each voter may vote for any one whom he or she pleases by writing in the name on the ballot. All annual elections shall be by written ballot, a majority of the ballots cast being necessary for the election of any officer. No voting by proxy shall be allowed.

Section 4: Vacancies

Vacancies occurring during the year may be filled for the unexpired term at any business meeting. The Advisory Council shall present to the Church nominees for the vacancies to be filled.

ARTICLE XII

MEETINGS

Section 1: Worship Services

Public services shall be on each Lord's Day and the Youth Fellowship and Church School shall meet at times fixed by the Board of Christian Education and approved by the Advisory Council and the Church.

The Lord's Supper shall be celebrated on the first Sunday of each month, and at such other times as the Church may determine.

Occasional religious meetings may be scheduled by the Pastor, by the Advisory Council, or by the vote of the Church.

Section 2: Business Meetings
The annual Business Meeting shall be on the second Friday evening in January for the purpose of receiving the annual reports of individual officers, boards, and committees of the Church, and its auxiliary organizations; the election of officers; and the transaction of such other business as is proper to come before this meeting.

Quarterly Advisory Council meetings shall be held in April, July, and October, on the Friday evening following the first Sunday thereof.

Fifteen members of the Advisory Council shall constitute a quorum.

Twenty-five members in good standing, qualified voters, shall constitute a quorum for the transaction of business.

Special business meetings may be called at any time by the Pastor or by the Clerk or by five (5) members in good standing who are qualified voters. Notices of such meeting and the object for which it is called shall be given on the Sunday preceding the date of the meeting. At any of the regular meetings of worship, however, the Church may, without notice, act upon the reception of members, upon the dismission of members to other churches, and upon the appointment of delegates to councils, associations, and Conventions, but not upon extraordinary business.

ARTICLE XIII

CHURCH YEAR

The fiscal year of the Church shall be the calendar year.

ARTICLE XIV

RULES OF ORDER

Section 1
The Hiscox *Directory* is the book on which our Church is incorporated.

Section 2

The rules contained in *Robert's Rules of Order* shall govern the business proceedings of this Church in all cases where they are not inconsistent with this Constitution.

ARTICLE XV

AMENDMENTS

This Constitution may be amended at any regular or called business meeting of the Church by a two-thirds (2/3) vote of those present and voting, provided a quorum is present and voting, and that notice of such amendment, stating the proposed change, shall have been given from the pulpit on two (2) successive Sundays.

Notes

NOTES TO THE PREFACE

[1] Edna C. Wells, ed., *Leon H. Sullivan: Philosophy of a Giant* (Philadelphia: Progressive Ventures Printers, Inc., 1973), p. 29.

[2] Charles Wesley, "A Charge to Keep I Have," *Baptist Standard Hymnal* (Nashville: Sunday School Publishing Board, National Baptist Convention, U.S.A., Inc.), p. 387.

[3] *Ibid.*

[4] Mary E. Goodwin, "Racial Roots and Religion—An Interview with Howard Thurman," *The Christian Century,* May 9, 1973, p. 535. Copyright 1973 by Christian Century Foundation. Reprinted by permission.

[5] Opinion expressed by Claude William Black, Jr., pastor, Mount Zion First Baptist Church, San Antonio, Texas, April, 1970.

[6] Based on personal correspondence between Elder B. Hicks, Regional Executive Minister, American Baptist Churches of the South, and the writers. Permission secured to use portions of his letter of February 5, 1974.

[7] Based on personal conversation with Lucius M. Tobin, retired Professor of Religion at Morehouse College and the Interdenominational Theological Center, Atlanta, Georgia, May 21, 1974.

NOTES TO CHAPTER 1

[1] James Haskins, *Witchcraft, Mysticism and Magic in the Black World* (New York: Doubleday & Company, Inc., 1974), p. 13.

[2] Charles J. Sargent, Jr., *Negro Churches and the American Baptist Convention,* speech delivered May 11, 1966, at American Baptist Convention, Kansas City, Missouri.

[3] Edward A. Freeman, *The Epoch of Negro Baptists and the Foreign Mission Board* (Kansas City: Central Seminary Press, 1953), pp. 23-24.

[4] *Ibid.,* p. 24.

[5] B. E. Mays and J. W. Nicholson, *The Negro's Church* (New York: Negro Universities Press, 1973), p. 3.

[6] Louis E. Lomax, *The Negro Revolt* (New York: Harper & Row, Publishers, 1962), p. 46.

[7] Wade Hampton McKinney, "A Study of the Negro Baptist Groups in the United States" (Bachelor of Divinity thesis, Rochester Theological Seminary, 1923), p. 32.

[8] *Ibid.,* pp. 34-35.

[9] Based on personal conversation with Kofi Asare Opoku, Research Fellow in Religion and Ethics, Institute of African Studies, University of Ghana at Legon, faculty member of the Martin Luther King, Jr., Program in Black Church Studies, Rochester, New York, August 2, 1974.

[10] Miles Mark Fisher, *Negro Slave Songs in the United States* (New York: The Citadel Press, 1953), pp. 27, 32-33.

[11] Kofi Asare Opoku.

[12] Kofi Asare Opoku.

[13] Thelma C. D. Adair, Professor of Education, Queens College, New York, N.Y., and Faculty/Consultant, Martin Luther King, Jr., Program in Black Church Studies.

[14] Opinion expressed by O. L. Sherman, retired African Methodist Church bishop in a sermon delivered to the Texas A.M.E. Educational Conference in Waco, Texas, July, 1974.

NOTES TO CHAPTER 2

[1] Ira De Augustine Reid, *The Negro Baptist Ministry* (Philadelphia: H and L Advertising Co., 1951), p. 133.

[2] Kofi Asare Opoku.

[3] Reid, *op. cit.,* p. 133.

[4] Opinion expressed by Gardner C. Taylor, pastor, Concord Baptist Church of Christ, Brooklyn, New York, and Past President, Progressive National Baptist Convention, Inc.

[5] John Gunther, *Inside Africa* (New York: Harper & Row, Publishers, 1953, 1954, 1955), pp. 820-821.

[6] Opinion expressed by Miles Mark Fisher, deceased, former pastor, White Rock Baptist Church, Durham, North Carolina.

[7] Opinion expressed by Wade H. McKinney, deceased, former pastor, Antioch Baptist Church, Cleveland, Ohio, November, 1954.

[8] Opinion expressed by Sandy F. Ray, pastor, Cornerstone Baptist Church, Brooklyn, New York; president, Empire State Baptist Convention of New York.

[9] Opinion expressed by Elliott J. Mason, Sr., pastor, Trinity Baptist Church, Los Angeles, California, and faculty member of the Martin Luther King, Jr., Program in Black Church Studies.

[10] Opinion expressed by O. Clay Maxwell, Sr., deceased, former pastor, Mt. Olivet Baptist Church, New York, New York; past president, Sunday School and Baptist Training Union, Congress of the National Baptist Convention, U.S.A., Inc.

[11] Based on personal conversation between Wade H. McKinney, deceased, former pastor, Antioch Baptist Church, Cleveland, Ohio, and one of the writers.

[12] Opinion expressed by Milton King Curry, Jr., President of Bishop College, Dallas, Texas, at school's Alumni Breakfast, National Baptist Convention, U.S.A., Inc., session held in Cleveland, Ohio, September, 1971.

[13] E. T. Hiscox, *The New Directory for Baptist Churches* (Valley Forge: Judson Press, 1894) and Henry M. Robert, *Robert's Rules of Order* (Chicago: Scott, Foresman and Company, 1951).

[14] James H. Cone, *Black Theology and Black Power* (New York: The Seabury Press, Inc., 1969), pp. 92-93.

[15] Edward A. Freeman, *The Epoch of Negro Baptists and the Foreign Mission Board* (Kansas City: Central Seminary Press, 1953), p. 23.

[16] Cone, *op. cit.,* p. 106.

[17] Opinion expressed by one of the writers, Samuel B. McKinney, on several occasions.

[18] Charles J. Sargent, Jr., *Negro Churches and the American Baptist Convention,* speech delivered May 11, 1966, at American Baptist Convention, Kansas City, Missouri.

[19] *Ibid.*

[20] Cornish L. Rogers, "Blacks and the Feminists," *Christian Century* (February 13, 1974), p. 172.

[21] Kofi Asare Opoku.

[22] Kofi Asare Opoku.

[23] Kofi Asare Opoku.

[24] Kofi Asare Opoku.

[25] Reid, *op. cit.*

[26] From personal correspondence between E. B. Hicks and the writers.

[27] Opinion expressed by B. J. Perkins, deceased, former pastor, Friendship Baptist Church, Cleveland, Ohio, and former treasurer of the National Baptist Convention, U.S.A., Inc., in dialogue years ago at the Baptist Ministers' Conference of Cleveland, Ohio, and vicinity.

[28] Opinion expressed by Louis Boddie, deceased, former pastor, Greater Harvest Baptist Church, Chicago, Illinois.

NOTES TO CHAPTER 3

[1] Based on personal conversation between Elliott J. Mason, Sr., pastor, Trinity Baptist Church, Los Angeles, California; faculty member of the Martin Luther King, Jr., Program on Black Church Studies, and the writers in Rochester, New York, July, 1974.

[2] Based on narrative prepared by Leon C. Jones, Area Minister, American Baptist Churches of the Northwest, former pastor, Second Baptist Church, Everett, Washington, and submitted to the writers, June, 1974.

[3] Opinion expressed by Louis Smith, Executive Director of OPERATION BOOTSTRAP, Los Angeles, California, faculty member of the Martin Luther King, Jr., Program in Black Church Studies in Rochester, New York, July, 1974.

NOTES TO CHAPTER 4

[1] Based on personal conversation between William Augustus Jones, Jr., pastor, Bethany Baptist Church, Brooklyn, New York, Martin Luther King, Jr., Fellow in Black Church Studies, and the writers in Rochester, New York, August, 1974.

[2] Based on personal conversation between Elliott J. Mason, Sr., pastor, Trinity Baptist Church, Los Angeles, California, faculty member of the Martin Luther King, Jr., Program in Black Church Studies and the writers in Rochester, New York, July, 1974.

[3] Based on personal conversation between Henry H. Mitchell, Director of the Martin Luther King, Jr., Program in Black Church Studies and the writers in Rochester, New York, July, 1974.

[4] Based on personal conversation between Kelly Miller Smith, Sr., pastor, First Baptist Church-Capitol Hill, Nashville, Tennessee, associate dean, Divinity School, Vanderbilt University, Nashville, Tennessee, and the writers in Philadelphia, Pennsylvania, May, 1974.

[5] Thomas Elliott Huntley, *Huntley's Manual for Every Baptist* (St. Louis, Mo.: Central Service Publication, 1963), p. 60.

[6] *Ibid.,* p. 61.

[7] Norton F. Brand and Verner M. Ingram, *The Pastor's Legal Advisor* (Nashville: Abingdon Press, 1942), p. 52.

[8] Edward T. Hiscox, *The New Directory for Baptist Churches* (Valley Forge: Judson Press, 1894), p. 117.

[9] Based on personal conversation between Louis Smith, Executive Director, OPERATION BOOTSTRAP, Los Angeles, California, faculty member of the Martin Luther King, Jr., Program in Black Church Studies and the writers in Rochester, New York, August, 1974.

NOTES TO CHAPTER 5

[1] Opinion expressed by Mary O. Ross, president, The Women's Auxiliary, National Baptist Convention, U.S.A., Inc., at Woman's Day Luncheon at the Mount Zion Baptist Church, Seattle, Washington, April, 1967.

NOTES TO CHAPTER 6

[1] Joseph R. Washington, Jr., "The Black Religious Crisis," *The Christian Century,* May 1, 1974, p. 475. Copyright 1974 by Christian Century Foundation. Reprinted by permission.

[2] Leon H. Sullivan, *Alternatives to Despair* (Valley Forge: Judson Press, 1972), pp. 109-110.

NOTES TO CHAPTER 7

[1] "Only Six Million Acres: The Decline of Black-Owned Land in the Rural South," Robert S. Browne, ed. Report sponsored by Clark College, Atlanta, Georgia, funded by The Rockefeller Brothers' Fund. (New York: The Black Economic Research, June, 1973), p. 1.

NOTES TO CHAPTER 8

[1] Based on personal conversation between Thelma C. Adair, Professor of Education, Queens College, New York, New York; faculty member of the Martin Luther King, Jr., Program in Black Church Studies, and the writers in Rochester, New York, August, 1974.

[2] Based on personal conversation between Robert F. Penn, Professor of Church Administration, Interdenominational Theological Center, Atlanta, Georgia, and the writers in Atlanta, Georgia, July, 1973.

NOTES TO CHAPTER 9

[1] Based on personal correspondence between Archie Smith, Jr., Associate Dean, Clark University, Worcester, Massachusetts, and the writers. Permission secured to use portions of his letter of January 6, 1975.

[2] *Ibid.*

[3] *Ibid.*

[4] Opinion expressed by Louis Smith, Executive Director, OPERATION BOOT-STRAP, Los Angeles, California, and faculty member of the Martin Luther King, Jr., Program in Black Church Studies.

[5] *Ibid.*

[6] *Ibid.*

[7] Opinion expressed by Thomas Kilgore, Jr., pastor, Second Baptist Church, Los Angeles, California, to the writers, August, 1974.

[8] *Ibid.*

[9] Archie Smith, Jr.

[10] *Ibid.*

[11] Opinion expressed by George B. Thomas, Martin Luther King, Jr., Fellow in Black Church Studies, in a sermon at the University of Ghana at Legon, Ghana, West Africa, August, 1972.

Index